AF709814

THE MAXIMAL IMPLICATIONS OF THE MINIMAL LINE

EXHIBITION CURATOR: LINDA WEINTRAUB

PUBLISHED BY THE EDITH C. BLUM ART INSTITUTE
MILTON AND SALLY AVERY CENTER FOR THE ARTS
THE BARD COLLEGE CENTER
ANNANDALE-ON-HUDSON, NEW YORK

Acknowledgments

Traveling back several decades into the careers of the artists in this exhibition has been a rewarding exploration.

It was motivated by a desire to supply young artists and art historians with their first opportunity to gain direct exposure to the art of the Minimalist era. Working with the artists, the lenders, the scholars, the donors, colleagues at Bard College, and consultants has provided me with a rare insight into the breadth of ideas that were spawned and proliferated by the Minimal aesthetic. The assembled body of work in this exhibition, however, goes beyond the mere return and reappraisal of a historic period. It provides irrefutable evidence of the inexhaustive resources of the artistic imagination in general. It is hoped that this exhibition will serve as a testimony to both.

The Maximal Implications of the Minimal Line is the summation of the numerous efforts and skills of talented individuals. Gratitude is extended to:

Advisors and Consultants:

Ben Boretz

Regina Cornwell

Elizabeth Goldring

Jon Hendricks

Robert Kelly

Donald Kuspit

George Quasha

Donna de Salvo

Phyllis Tuchman

John Weber

Bard College Staff:

Dimitri Papadimitriou, Executive Vice President

Iris Kufert, Assistant to the Director

Mirko Gabler, Preparator

Lucy Ferriss, Director of Publications

Judy Samoff, Director of Grants

Ann Gabler-Gourlay, Program Development Associate

Elizabeth Shea, Director of Central Services

Tina Iraca Green, Director of Public Relations

Richard Griffiths, Director of Physical Plant

Donald Bennett, Dining Services Manager

Jeffrey Gillis, Director of Audio Visuals

Donors:

New York State Council on the Arts

National Endowment for the Arts

Spectra-Physics

Meet the Composer

Lenders:

Art Gallery of Ontario

Blum Helman Gallery

Leo Castelli Gallery

Paula Cooper Gallery

Charles Cowles Gallery

DIA Foundation

Mr. Norman Dolph

Mr. Gerald Elliot

The Elkon Gallery, Inc.

Ronald Feldman, Fine Arts

Xavier Fourcade Gallery, Inc.

Barbara Gladstone

Michael Klein, Inc.

David Lichtenstein

Jane Logemann and Gerry Rosen

Herbert Lust

Cintra Murray

National Gallery of Canada/ Galerie Nationale du Canada

The Pace Gallery

Parrish Art Museum

Stuart Rickey

The Gilbert and Lila Silverman Fluxus Collection

Holly and Horace Solomon

Sonnabend Gallery

Washburn Gallery

John Weber Gallery

Artists' Collections

—Linda Weintraub
Curator

Board of Trustees Bard College:

William F. Rueger, *Chairman emeritus*
David E. Schwab II, *Chairman*
Sally M. Avery, *Honorary Trustee*
Leon Botstein, *President, Bard College*
Jean de Castella de Delley
Asher Edelman
Jerome I. Feldman
Alan R. Finberg
Eric Warren Goldman
Elizabeth Blodgett Hall
Ernest Henderson III
John C. Honey
Charles S. Johnson III
Mark N. Kaplan
Lydia P. S. Katzenbach
Leon Levy
The Rt. Rev. Paul Moore, Jr.
Hart Perry, *Treasurer*
Thom Mount
The Hon. Ogden R. Reid
Charles P. Stevenson, Jr.
Peter H. Stone
Robert B. Strassler
Paul W. Williams, *Trustee emeritus*

Board of Overseers Edith C. Blum Art Institute:

Dore Ashton
Sally M. Avery
Isabel Bishop
Leon Botstein, *ex officio*
Arnold Davis
Jean de Castella de Delley
Asher Edelman
Frances Friedman
Wilbur Friedman, *Chair*
Eric W. Goldman
Barbara Haskell
Stephen Mazoh
Harvey Miller
Dimitri Papadimitriou, *ex officio*
Beatrice Perry
Judith Rothschild
Linda Weintraub, *ex officio*
Tom Wolf, *Faculty Representative*

Board of Trustees The Bard College Center:

The Hon. Ogden R. Reid, *Founding Chairman*
Sally M. Avery, *Chair*
John Holden Adams
Helen Bernstein
Leon Botstein, *President, Bard College*
Jean de Castella de Delley
Eric W. Goldman
Helen Hayes
John C. Honey
Leon Levy
John V. Lindsay
Jack McEnroe
Kenneth Miron
Roy R. Neuberger
Dimitri Papadimitriou, *Executive Director*
Joseph Papp
Martin Peretz
David Rose
John C. Sawhill
Hilton Weiss, *Faculty Representative*

Copyright © Bard College, 1985

All rights reserved

Published by Bard College
Edith C. Blum Art Institute
Annandale-on-Hudson, NY

Catalog design: Anthony McCall Associates, New York
Printed at Studley Press

Library of Congress Catalogue Card Number: #84-073340
ISBN: #0-941276-06-6
Edition limited to 2,500 copies

This exhibition has been organized in part with public funds from the National Endowment for the Arts and the New York State Council on the Arts.

Table of Contents

Introduction
Linda Weintraub

In selecting a single straight line as the formal denominator which unites the works of the fifty-eight artists included in this exhibition, the aim was to dramatize the essential character of an entire era in the art of the recent past. Minimalism was the aesthetic code which dominated much of the art scene throughout the 1960s and 1970s. The pursuit of simplicity of form was carried to its logical extreme by a whole generation of artists who considered any image that strayed from extreme reduction a violation of the moral integrity of art and contemptible pretension. Their work was carried on with missionary zeal, and the contest over who made the first all-white canvas, the first cube sculpture, and, perhaps, the first work of art consisting of a single straight line has been fought only because credit and honor is expected to accrue to the individual identified in each case.

To many observers whose tastes and expectations about art were formulated prior to this period, and to the generation of artists who are too young to have either witnessed or participated in this race toward reductive extremism, the Minimalist era seems to have been dismissed with the most casual of gestures as sterile and boring. They have come to associate simplicity of form with artlessness, banality, and monotony.

The purpose of this exhibition is to reassemble notable members of the art world whose work was infused with the formal restraints of Minimalism, even if this label is not otherwise associated with them. The Minimal aesthetic swept the era otherwise characterized by its pluralism. It became integrated into the other "isms" that coexisted throughout these years. These movements were represented in this exhibition in order to reveal Minimalism's ubiquitous presence. The show includes examples of performance art, conceptual art, kinetic art, environmental art, earth art, and process art.

In order to make explicit the formal restraint that unites them all, every work of art in this show was selected because it consists of a single straight line. This format describes the single most elementary visual unit. It is the building block from which all other shapes are derived; curved, bent, multiplied, it generates the universe of forms. As such, the solitary line serves to focus attention on the most controversial aspect of Minimalism.

It is hoped that the profusion of varied and distinct art objects in this exhibition will serve as a testimony to the intensity of creative activity that the Minimalist creed

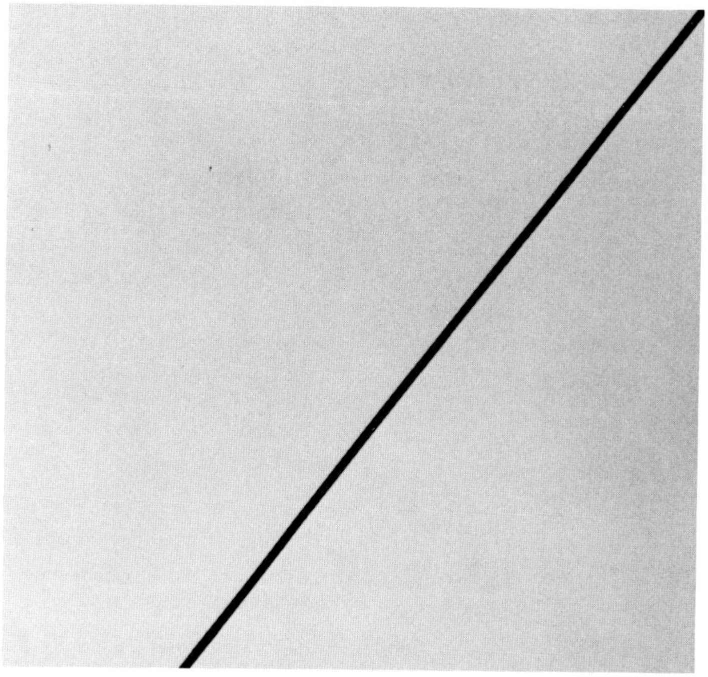

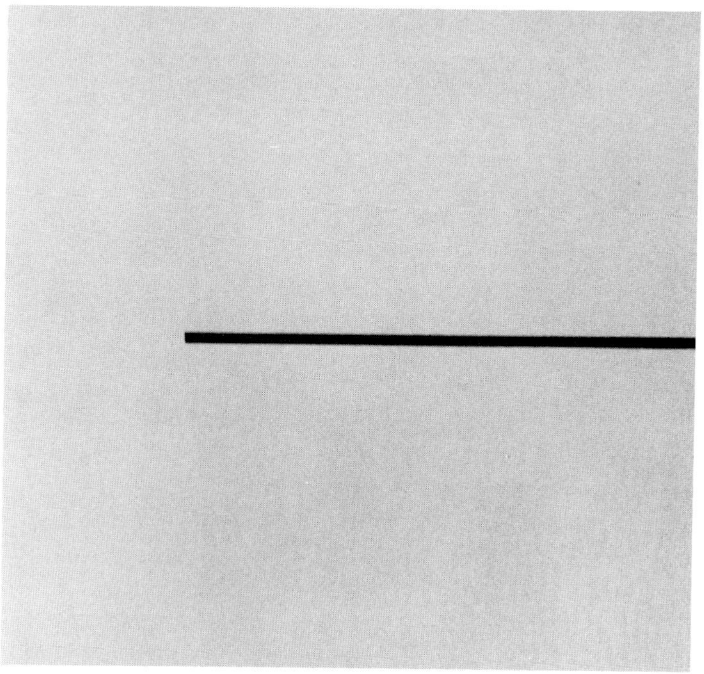

Ellsworth Kelly. Top: *Diagonal,* 1951. (Drawing from proposed book by artist in 1951, "Line, Form and Color"). Ink; 7½ × 8″. Collection of the artist. Bottom: *Horizontal Line,* 1951. (Drawings from proposed book by artist in 1951, "Line, Form and Color"). Ink; 7½ × 8″. Collection of the artist.

serviced, if not engendered. Within the humble confines of a single line, an entire generation discovered a wealth of options. It was charged, by these artists, to convey concepts, objects, forces, gender, weight, emotion, wit, humor, elegance, and banality. What unites the works of art in this exhibition is the audacious exploration of the words "much" and "little" as they apply to art. Each embodies a search for absolutes and a probing of the outer limits. The implicit qualities of the line itself mirrors the contradiction between Minimalism's apparent simplicity and its conceptual complexity, its formal monotony and its manifest diversity. For instance, a line has but one dimension. It is unequivocal and pure, and is so elemental that it can be apprehended in its entirety, immediately. Artists who employ this format as the sole element in a work of art have drastically reduced the number of aesthetic decisions required of them. Shape is predetermined, and the problems of illusion, composition, design, and symmetry have all been obviated. The work can have neither climax nor focus, and opportunity for imitation is denied. Indeed, concentration on pure geometry, and the concomitant restrictions on the process of creation just described, are essential characteristics of all Minimal art. It undermines the traditional belief in art as the cherished domain of free creative expression. It is the realization of this new definition that has caused some individuals to think of Minimalism as the negation of art, a nihilistic gesture. But in choosing to refrain from some activities, Minimal artists were able to affirm other ideas. They welcomed the confines of this irreducible image, and undertook the task of exploring, to the point of exhaustion, all the options that it offered.

Depending on how it is presented, a line can appear monumental, minute, or scaleless. It can be scribed with pencil, pen, or brush, or realized in neon, laser, wood, brick, rope, earth, gauze, film, pipe, girder, or beam. Its form can emerge from cutting, folding, projecting, or simply thinking. In one instance it may be a record of a human gesture. In another it is the result of industrial fabrication.

Lines can hang, lean, lie, or tilt. They can succumb to the force of gravity or, in a diagonal orientation, imply motion, velocity, and direction. Throughout, lines either assume the role of metaphor, or they exist as literal, nonreferential objects in the real world. As a result, limiting the aesthetic vocabulary to a single straight line has not prevented these artists from exploring distant extremes of creative possibility. On the one hand, some Minimal artists have elected to exploit the initial reduction of the single line format. They have pursued ways to further restrict and purify the art object. Others have sought devices to load this elemental, and essentially neutral format, with content.

The artists in the first category, such as Carl Andre, Fred Sandback, Sol LeWitt, and John McCracken, have increased the previously described list of omissions. These hermetic Minimalists also relinquished gesture, movement, texture, color, metaphor, self-expression, light, space, emotion, illusion, ambiguity, and craftsmanship. They pursued anonymity and sterility as a positive goal reflective of such virtues as rationality, truth, and verifiability. This art served to deliver the viewer from delusion, in the same way that data and scientific facts can be known with comforting certainty.

The terms that were invented to designate this kind of art as it was first emerging reveal the varying attitudes with which it was received. What some identified as unmitigated banality, others perceived as righteous purity. Irving Sandler spoke of "one shot art" and "cool art," while Clement Greenberg invented the term "post painterly abstraction" to describe these "primary structures." Michael Fried preferred the word "literalism," and Barbara Rose coined the term "ABC Art."

In all, these artists gave new meaning to the terms geometry, abstraction, and formalism. They established a discomfiting new relationship between the art object and the viewer, one in which the opportunity for sensual or spiritual rapport was categorically denied. The Minimal object was inert, self-enclosed and non-engaging. As a result, the relationship between art and criticism underwent equally fundamental changes. The purpose of the Minimal art object was to embody clarity. All the essential elements were made explicit; discussion and analysis were preempted.

In the other category belong those artists who perceived in the reduction to elemental formal elements, a challenge to the creative imagination. They have interjected the ambiguity and subjectivity that promotes interpretation and narrative elements. There is a tension in their work between the conceptual and the perceptual elements of a single line. Hans Haacke has used it to make manifest the constant fluctuations in environmental conditions. Michelle Stuart's line recalls ecological transformations. In Chris Burden's piece, it becomes a trajectory plotting fear, danger, and vulnerability. To Douglas Huebler, it is a poignant link between the viewer and the rotation of the globe on its axis. For Mel Bochner, it serves as a conveyor of systems of logic, and to John Baldessari, it embodies a futile action. In each of these examples, and in manifold others, the line does not describe an object. Its function bypasses description to embrace expanded facts and fictions.

In the essays that follow, the long trend toward simplification and the search for essentialization in the art of this century are carefully plotted. Looking back, beginning with the generation of the Bauhaus, the Constructiv-

Ellsworth Kelly. *Horizontal Band (1),* 1951. Collage; 4⅞ × 6½". Collection of the artist.

Ellsworth Kelly. *Horizontal Band,* 1951. Collage; 7½ × 8". Collection of the artist.

ists, and the Neoplasticists, extending through the work of Clyfford Still, Ad Reinhardt, Ellsworth Kelly, Barnett Newman, and Kenneth Noland, the succession of styles seems irrevocable, and the culmination into Minimalism appears a historical necessity. Minimal art was the grand fulfillment of the requisites proposed by these predecessors: conceptual clarity, precise means, and a literal confrontation with the physical reality of art.

In order to identify Minimal art as a cultural phenomenon as revealing of our century as Baroque or Mannerist art was capable of conveying the historic essence of the 16th and 17th centuries, it is essential that the reader be aware of the inevitability describing Minimalism's reduction of formal elements can be repeated as it is applied to each of the other art forms. Indeed, even the utilization of a single straight line is shared by poets, musicians, dancers, and filmmakers throughout the era of the 1960s and 1970s: La Monte Young's *Draw a Straight Line and Follow It* and his composition *B and F Sharp,* Steve Reich's *Pendulum Piece,* Nam June Paik's *Zen for Film,* Pauline Oliveros's *Sonic Meditations,* John Cage's *Empty Words,* Terry Riley's *In C,* Alvin Lucier's *Music on a Long Thin Wire,* Paul Sharritt's *Stream, Section, Stream,* Anthony McCall's *Four Projected Movements,* Jackson MacLow's *Tree Movie,* Robert Kelly's *Axon Dendron Tree,* Simone Forti's *Huddle,* Michael Snow's *Wavelength.* Each of these individuals validates the work of the others. As a total cultural expression, they both describe and define an era that embraced extremism in its dedication to pursuing, to its logical conclusion, the innovations of their predecessors. The spirit and significance of this pursuit is presented in this exhibition as a metaphor: the maximal implications of the minimal line.

The Minimalist Line as an Attenuated, Tragic Act of Art, *Donald Kuspit*

"So, if in the picture the line is freed from the aim of designating a thing and functions as a thing itself, its inner resonance is not weakened by any subordinate roles and acquires its full inner strength."
Wassily Kandinsky, *On the Problem of Form* (1912)

"The tragic adheres to all form and natural color, for the struggle for freedom is expressed by the tensing of line and the intensification of color as a striving against a stronger counter-striving. Only when line is tensed to the rectilinear and naturalistic color is intensified to pure plane-color—only then can tragic expression be reduced to a minimum."
Piet Mondrian, *From the Natural to the Abstract: From the Indeterminate to the Determinate* (1918)

". . . whereas the curved line was used predominantly for reasons of beauty (Phidias, Michelangelo, Raphael, Rubens) it has been used more and more economically for reasons of truth (Millet, Monet, Cézanne) until it will end as the straight line for reasons of Love. This will enable the art of the future to create an international form; a form understandable to all and vital enough to the expression of a general feeling of love in a monumental way. Such is the future."
Theo van Doesburg, *Remarks on Art* (1914)

"The straight line corresponds to the velocity of modern traffic. . . ."
Theo van Doesburg, *Elementarism and Its Origins,* (1928)

"I call the additional element of Suprematism 'the suprematist straight line' (dynamic in character). The environment corresponding to this new culture has been produced by the latest achievements of technology. . . ."
Kasimir Malevich, *Introduction to the Theory of the Additional Element in Painting* (1927)

"The straight line tells the truth, and the meaning you want it to have is of no value for painting; such significance is literary, didactic."
Piet Mondrian, *A Dialogue on Neoplasticism* (1919)

Is Minimalism—at its most minimalist in the (mostly) straight line—the realization of Van Doesburg's dream of the future, the heir of Suprematism, Neoplasticism, Elementarism? Has Minimalism eliminated the tragic? Is this the reason it has so often been pejoratively described as cold, inhuman, "puritan"? Do these terms represent a misreading of what is actually a triumph of art, the realization of one of the deepest modernist ambitions, and a profound metaphoric statement of what it is to be authentically human: to live without tragedy? To evolve, through aesthetics, beyond tragedy, so that tragic existence becomes an anachronism: does this not reveal the full extent of the modernist belief in art's power? Does it not reveal the intention that is usually unacknowledged—repressed—but secretly motivates the best modernist activity, and has at last become fully explicit in Minimalism, the most profoundly Elementaristic of all modernist arts?

Mondrian wrote: "So long as art continues to use natural appearance as its plastic means, its expression will *emphasize the tragic*."[1] Mondrian thought that "the tragic will be transcended"—"emotion subordinated to the natural . . . will become spiritual emotion"—when "the outward will be in equilibrium with the inward in consciousness."[2] The work of art allegorically represents this spiritual equilibrium "through the exact, *equilibrated* plastic of relationship," in which *"unity in the expression of content and its appearance"* is achieved through "equilibrium of position and size."[3] But such unity is purely aesthetic, whatever spiritual unity it symbolizes—purely a matter of culture, not of nature, which are, as Mondrian believed, always in opposition. A cultural achievement does not change a natural reality. Thus, to be human is always to be partially tragic, for the human remains natural however spiritual it becomes—however much it uses culture to transcend its natural condition. That condition can never be totally—only partially, idealistically—transcended. The aesthetic is a form of idealistic thinking, in which the outward and the inward are unified as in fact they never can be in experience. The human remains residually tragic because it is explicitly bound to the bodily, however spiritual emotion becomes. Even such a determined spritualist as Mondrian acknowledges as much: "the tragic *in nature is manifested as corporeality*."[4] This implicitly recognizes that the corporeal inherently lacks equilibrium. And it implies that as long as art remains corporeal—"natural"—it remains immanently tragic. The Minimalist line is secretly tragic, because it remains very material—powerfully material, as we will see from many of the works in the exhibition—even when it seems immaterial, that is, represents absolutely spiritual emotion. In fact, it is just when it seems to do so that it reveals how thoroughly embedded in material—how heavily dependent upon the material—it is. The inescapable conclusion is that Minimalism is the subtlest tragic art there is—the art in which the tragically human is revealed most nakedly, in the simplest of geometrical gestures.

But let us begin by arguing the other way—by accepting the Minimalist assumption that it refines the art object to a limit beyond which it cannot go without disintegrating into what is a non-art object, articulates it as an even more basic, perfected, dynamic equilibrium than that proposed by Mondrian. Through our acceptance we will discover how Minimalism contradicts—undermines—itself; unwittingly, by reason of the ambiguity of its own premises, it becomes the profoundest expression of modern art—exactly the opposite of what it intended to be. It becomes the major signifier of the near impossibility—if not mortality—of art in modern administered society, a society which administers objects as well as people.[5] It preempts all critical—"free"—will, including the will to art. Part of Minimalism's tragic character is that it can be understood as showing, more than any other art made today, the scars on the will to art that come from art's trying to hold its own in the administered world. With its preconceived ideas of what art should be—its attempt to set limits on and thus appropriate "avant-garde" art, control the very destiny of art—the culture industry curbs the will to art, forces it to heel like a dog. Minimalism is a tragic survivor of this world, an art that refuses to conform yet that is peculiarly inhibited, implying that it has internalized the social restraints on it. It signifies a manqué will to art—a peculiarly self-effacing however heroic and resilient (resistant to appropriation) will to art. Minimalism escapes from the stereotype of what art should be by effacing its own will to art, which is the measure of its desperation. Like all survivors, it exists reduced to fundamental terms: both its self-effacement and the determination of its will to art are reflected in its fundamentalist aesthetic. This fundamentalism, the very instrument of its survival, is in danger of seeming hollow in the culture industry, but it also affords a rudimentary integrity: the only way to survive in the administered world is to travel light—but that may be to become light. This is Minimalism's inherent ambiguity and tragedy. It reflects the will to art victimized by the culture industry that controls the concept and production of art, but the fundamentalist terms it uses to rebel against and escape from control are self-victimizing, suggest a masochistic will to art. Fundamentalism in general is always as inhibiting as it is integrating—as much a sign of damaged will as a forced march to integrity.

Minimalism, then, can be understood as carrying the idea of art as the articulation and mastery of equilibrated relationship to its logical conclusion. The form of the equilibrium is reduced to a minimum, that is, to the absolute limit of form—a limit at which it is released from any resemblance to natural appearance, a limit at which it has at last relinquished any illusionistic potential, a limit which drains it of any gratuitous "expressivity." It is at this limit that Minimalism becomes "fundamentalist"—basic, universally legible art, the purified will to art. It is at this limit, towards which Minimalism strains with every bit of intellectual muscle, that tragic expression supposedly disappears, loses its irksome inevitability, apparently profound necessity as the ground of all expression. A post-tragic world of epiphanic aesthetic appearance emerges, releasing emotion from its naturalness. Emotional harmony follows from aesthetic harmony—from the simple, indissolubly harmonious straight line, articulated as the end product of an intense refining, and in the process unavoidable redefining, of plastic equilibrium. Indeed, it is the straight line, arrived at through the Minimalist pursuit of the irreducible, that more than any other shape has what Gabo described as "the emotional force of an absolute shape," that is, has "immediate, irresistible, and universal" effect.[6] What greater harmony is there than that expressed by the straight line, which is completely non-natural—never really exists in nature? It is Platonically intelligible, embodying ideal unity, complete absence of contradiction—unconditional harmony—that makes nature seem completely beside the point, irreversibly transcended. The straight line seems the true emissary of eternity. The Renaissance notion that a great artist shows himself by being able to draw a perfect circle freehand must no doubt be superseded by the Minimalist presupposition that an artist shows his stature by being able to pull a straight line out of nature and make it leap beyond nature. It is this leap of intellectual faith that is the heart of Minimalism.

Further elaborating his sense of the tragic and its "resolution," Mondrian wrote: "No matter how the duality of inward and outward is manifested—as nature and spirit, man against man, male and female, *or* in art as the plastic against representational content—so long as this duality has not achieved equilibrium and recovered its unity, it remains *tragic.* If this duality in art requires equivalent *plastic expression,* then the artist must be able to abolish tragic expression (so far as this is possible)."[7]

Why the qualifying clause—the hesitancy—about how far this is possible? Doesn't the straight line abolish the duality of tragic expression—the disequilibrium, conflict, disorder (all terms Mondrian used to describe the "overemphasis" on one term of an "opposition," usually the bodily term—reconciling the plastic and representational content, being both, that is, being both the purest (most non-natural, most purely presentational) plastic element and most subtle mimesis—"poetry"—of the intelligibility lurking in nature? Didn't Mondrian say that he "favors the straight line" because, "in searching for an expression of vastness [in nature], I was led to seek the *greatest* tension: the straight line, because all curvature resolves into the straight, no place remains for the curved?"[8]

It is not so simple. For the possibility of abolishing tragic expression in art is contingent upon—no doubt unexpectedly by disbelieving aesthetes—the possibility of living in a society free of tragedy. Supposedly autonomous art does not control its own destiny, its own content; it is less autonomous than it thinks, for it subtly reflects, if not necessarily the appearances of society, the will that makes it what it is. Even for Mondrian, the sense that society was moving toward—trying to will its own—equilibrium, was crucial. Abstractly equilibrated art had a social role to play; its very possibility was socially necessitated. The absence of the will to social equilibrium would haunt the equilibrium intended by his own art-making, the desire for equilibrium that was the raison d'etre of his will to art. It would be a crippled, insecure, even empty ("decorative") equilibrium that would result—an equilibrium that would reflect the ambiguous character of human will in the modern world in general—in a world that did not have any decisive will to harmony, that had even forgotten the meaning of and lost the intention to create harmony: a world that was irredeemably tragic, that was hardened to its own tragic reality.

Proto-Minimalist art proposed in modern form the age-old possibility of—hope for—the elimination of the tragic and the actualization of harmony. But it presented this profound yet familiar human ideal not simply in the traditional way, as an unconscious wish, implicitly unrealizable and despairing, but as a goal to be consciously and possibly successfully pursued—socially or realistically in sight. Social harmony was not simply a goal anxiously desired but one for which the instruments of realization actually existed. Elementaristic art could only have reaffirmed the goal in freshly concrete terms—rather than having naïvely reasserted it in the old mythical language—if modern society was ready for its realization. The modern validity of the goal of eliminating the tragic, not to speak of the seriousness with which the goal demanded to be taken, depends entirely on the means society has available to realize it. Mondrian's equilibrated art catalyzed fresh consciousness of the goal of social harmony because society no longer thought about it in futile utopian terms—self-consciously utopian terms that masked an unconscious feeling of futility and doubt that the goal could ever be realized.

Modern society has technology—the machine—and only it, as Van Doesburg wrote, can provide "constructive certainty. The new potentialities of the machine have given rise to an aesthetic theory appropriate to our age, which I have had occasion to call the 'mechanical aesthetic'."[9] The mechanical aesthetic bespeaks the goal of harmony, of freedom from tragedy; it implicitly idealizes the machine as if to enforce its socially constructive use. Its socially destructive, tragic use in World War I could not have been far from Van Doesburg's mind. It was as though history was at an especially decisive crossroads: it had, in the machine, the means of a more tragic existence—of totally destroying itself—than ever; or it had the means of creating a true, effective social harmony. The machine made possible the greatest tragedy or the greatest harmony, and the mechanical aesthetic, arising out of profound recognition, even homage, to the machine, was an attempt to morally influence it, and the social use to which it would be put, for the better. From the point of view of being modern, of making modern rather than traditional art, the mechanical aesthetic reflects an attitude to the machine not dissimilar from Malevich's insistence that Suprematism is inseparable from "the big city's metallic culture . . . of energy . . . machines, motors, and power lines."[10] The provincialism—"peace of the countryside"—this repudiates is equivalent to tradition, as well as the empty utopianism of the pastoral version of the wish for social harmony.

It must be emphasized that for Malevich and Van Doesburg, harmony—life without tragedy—was possible in life only to the extent technology made it possible. Technology was civilization's most concrete, practical attempt to transcend the tragic to date. Art mimicked and encouraged this attempt; it did not invent it, although it perhaps saw technology's potential for social good better than society as a whole, which seemed to have regarded the production of efficient instruments as an end in itself as well as a simplistic sign of modernity. It was partly because of his belief in technology that Malevich asserted that "art no longer cares to serve the state and religion, it no longer wishes to illustrate the history of manners."[11] Art now had a more important, truly modern task: to articulate the potentially harmonious use of technology in no uncertain terms—to unequivocally set a satisfactory social goal for technology. The state and religion had failed to create social harmony; the history of manners reflected this lack of social harmony. Technology was humanity's last chance to make peace with itself, to create a tranquil society, and art was going to play a crucial role in historically realizing once and for all this goal—and so in a sense ending history, ending conflict, implicitly ending the need for the state and religion as regulators or arbitrators of conflict. Art would focus the goal of harmony in clear and distinct plastic terms—"Cartesianism" in the service of social harmony. Art would function as technology's conscience, finding its own social value. Art would at last have a truly challenging "higher" social purpose, the authentic basis for a truly "higher" aesthetic. It would be both beautiful and truthful—exist for its own sake because it existed for society's sake. What an extraordinary goal: to liberate humanity from tragedy! And thereby to find its own authentically aesthetic destiny.

Minimalism shows that it could not be done. It shows art in a state of disbelief in and indifference to technology as well as the state and religion—in a state of disillusionment with the modern world as such. It shows idealistic, socially activist Elementaristic art turning into a matter-of-fact aesthetic fundamentalism that completely betrays—abandons—the cultural goals that inspired its originators. Minimalism shows the collapse of the modern dialectic—inherent to the very idea of modernism in art—between so-called art for art's sake and the social use of art. It represents the collapse of the belief system that attempted to reconcile the two—to establish a socially useful "absolute" art. "The shapes we are creating are not abstract, they are absolute," wrote Gabo. "By the influence of an absolute form the human psyche can be broken or molded."[12] An absolute form generates the emotion on which "the whole edifice or our everyday existence"—society—can be rebuilt, as well as through which opposing senses of art can be reconciled. The belief in the reciprocity of art and technology is one aspect of the larger belief in art's power over the "psychical forces" that shape existence. But when, through historical experience, the belief in this reciprocity collapses because of the human failure to create social harmony, the emotional hold of art over the psyche weakens. Minimalism represents the bankruptcy of the dream of the influence of absolute form on the psyche as well as on society—the recognition that absolute form is simply absolute form, with no implications beyond that of hermetic art. It has its place in the history of style, nowhere else. Mondrian's goal of an art free of "literary, didactic" purpose is ironically achieved.

But Mondrian did not go as far as Minimalism in repudiating "literary, didactic" purpose for art, in asserting aesthetic fundamentalism. (This was ironical; art consciously sought to abolish, by becoming absolute, what it unconsciously knew society had already denied it: significant influence on society and the psyche.) The same Mondrian who explicitly denied such purpose believed that *"simplicity,"* sign of the "new harmony, . . . will come automatically through the quest for efficiency in machinery, in transportation."[13] Even more didactically, Mondrian seemed to believe that in the modern world it is art, by reason of its power over the emotions—its power to transform natural into spiritual emotions—that first seriously proposes the goal of *"attaining equilibrium between nature and the non-natural*—between *what is in us and what is around us."* It is through technology that "(relative) equilibrium is *reached*" and art's "task will be fulfilled and harmony will be *realized* in our outward surroundings and in our outward life."[14] But it is art that first consciously articulated the goal of harmony in modern life by self-consciously realizing it in itself by transforming itself. It becomes exemplarily modern by positing harmony in the non-objective, "absolute" terms appropriate to the modern technological world. It was in such absolute art that the domination of the tragic first ended, preparing the way for the moment when "the domination of the tragic in life will be ended" and "the 'artist' will be absorbed by the 'fully human being'."[15] Minimalism, it seems, is the dregs of this absolute art—absolute art without its high cultural purpose, its socially symbolic import. Minimalism is absolute art become humanly meaningless.

But is it ever really possible to be either humanly meaningless (not representative of the human condition, human history) or "fully human," that is, free of the tragic, completely harmonious—on Mondrian's own premises? *"Because it is manifested plastically, the human spirit, which is expressed by aesthetic plastic, seeks its visual manifestation free of the tragic."*[16] But the human spirit, in its very plasticity, remains tragic—dualistic—at its core; it is always "naturally" set against itself. For its inherent plasticity, as well as its plastic manifestation, means its inherent physicality—the physical whose predominance in the masses Mondrian deplores,[17] but which he finds undeniable. In Minimalism the physical or bodily—the plastic as such—shows itself not in concrete color plasticity or the plasticity of the interaction of horizontal and vertical, as in Mondrian. These are not simply sharply reduced in Minimalism, but denied (the Neoplastic horizontal/vertical axes are dismembered by the destruction of spatial direction; color plasticity is simply dismissed). An absolutely "minimal," attenuated sense of the plastic is created, readable as the most elementary manifestation of the most primitive will to art. It is as though we are witnessing, in the minimal art work, human will at the moment it mutates into artistic will, revealing itself at its most naked. There is something peculiarly tragic about such a minimal thing or mark—line—being taken as the sign of absolute artistic will. It is as though what once operated from an economy of abundance now expresses an economy of scarcity. It is as though what was once determined to be enduring stoically accepts its own transience, becoming peculiarly poignant and pathetic.

The minimalist line, of all minimalist art objects, is precarious, reduces to a gesture, which, however grand, seems to exist in a vacuum, even represent a vacuum of meaning and intention, as well as of artistic method. It is weirdly tragic. No matter how intensified into straightness line is, it is by default—its own default—a tragic expression. But it is tragic in a new way: it does not represent duality, but the collapse of any drive to equilibrium, any will to unify opposites. It represents a nihilistic recognition and acceptance of social disharmony—the futility of ever achieving social harmony. It is the nihilistic opposite to Elementaristic art's "pragmatic" utopianism. That nihilism expresses not only the abandonment of any attempt by art to make itself socially useful, but also the abandonment of the goal of art for art's sake, belief in art's autonomy. The minimalist "desublimation" of art is double-edged: it implies the desublimation of absolute art—its abandonment as a vehicle for such sublime (because suppressed, merely lipserviced) intentions as social harmony—and the desublimation of art as such into an unenigmatic realm of ritualistic manipulations, a sort of "sociolinguistic" game of sound and fury signifying nothing. For it is not clear that the minimalist line articulates an intention that can be called "artistic" in the full sense of the word—brings forth worlds of form and meaning hitherto unsuspected, brings forth simply that plenitude which we call a world. At best, we know only that it is made by a human will, and located in a context of understanding called "art," a context increasingly hard to delimit and define, if transparently limited. Indeed, Minimalism seems to represent the limit of our difficulty with it. We fall back on our sense of this human will—so enfeebled that it does not know its own name, only what it can "act," make a minimal mark, take a minimal stand—to understand the minimalist line. It can only represent human will tragically dissociated from any sense of self—will that acts but does not know the ground and direction of its action, that is, that does not know its own intention, only that it must intend—must intend to be. It is clearly will that no longer expects to have any influence on the world—to be mirrored by it (or to want to mirror it). But this negativity shows its authentic "humanity"—suggests that it represents the basic state of modern humanity, so administered it does not know its own intentions, its own "subjectivity." It does not know the possibility of authentic self-reflection because of its tragic state, by reason of its being networked rather than reflected by the world.

"Art has the *intention,*" Mondrian wrote, "of plastically establishing complete freedom from the tragic: but its *expression,* the *plastic,* created by and for man, lags behind art's intention."[18] Even when its plastic expression is denaturalized, when "individuality is actually annihilated in expression" and "the universal has reached the masses," the unfreedom which the tragic is a sign of lurks within the freedom made possible by plastic equilibrium. For the intention to be free of tragic lack of equilibrium can never find its proper artistic expression without the human determination to be free, and, as Mondrian intimates, that determination is not socially encouraged. Art, for all its good intentions, remains subtly tragic, subtly subjective. In Minimalism the tension—opposition—between intention and expression has collapsed, leaving an unexpectedly completely subjective art—looking like a completely objective art—which hardly knows what its intention is, only that it intends to be "art." What that is, as we have indicated, is another, relatively unclear, matter. "*Although in Neoplasticism subjective vision is reduced to a minimum,* it nevertheless remains subjective and still must express something of the tragic. It does this through the rhythm of the composition."[19] The very dynamic through which opposites are equilibrated is the sign of the tragic subjectivity of art. The dynamic that is meant to "resolve" the human reveals it despite itself—reveals the modern form of its dualism. And Minimalism reveals the raw, indefensible human will, in the form of the raw will to art, even more absolutely.

My understanding of Minimalism is this: it carries to the furthest possible extreme the effort of Neoplasticism, and other kinds of non-objective or absolute art, the attempt to eliminate the tragic in art, but fails. It pushes the possibility of absolute art to the limit, but the tragic is implicit because the achievement of absolute art remains a subjective act. Its subtle subjectivity is more interesting than its unsubtle artistry, which seems on the verge of losing credibility as art, because it itself makes clear that the meaning of art is no longer clear. Minimalism is not simply the latest version of the old Duchampian game, but the articulation of the historical condition of both art and subjectivity, and their equivocal yet undeniable relationship. Subjectivity as well as art is vanishing, yet remains, not simply as haunting absence but as the presence of vanishing, "minimal" art.

Minimalism, like Pop art, its peer, seems to have as its project the elimination or at least scaling—whittling—down of subjectivity, even the demonstration that it is an illusion. Pop art has the ironic ideal of the machine-made look—which shows just how absurdly far the De Stijl belief in reconciliation with the machine has gone. Yet this absurdity reflects the truth of modern life, dominated by the pursuit of objectivity—of being object-like. Pop art shows that the subject could never come together with the object on equal footing—there is greater respect for the object than the subject in modern life (unless the subject can be shown to be object-like). The subject always remains submissive to the object in the administered modern world, with its implicit goal that everyone must be like a machine, or fit in "the machine"—the System. Minimalism is not unrelated to Pop art in that it shows what is left of the subject—in the form of the will to art—in the completely administered (machine-like) world envisioned by Pop art. (For all its supposed ironic, critical resistance to and manipulation of the media in the name of some subliminal notion of the "free" subject, Pop art is dominated by the machine-like—manufactured—look which it creates [implying a mechanical understanding of the world, which usually implies an acceptance of its status quo]. Pop art is more manipulated than manipulative of the media, the most obvious instance of the System—of administered thinking and appearance.)

When Robert Morris, in his minimalist phase, argued that Minimalism attempts to engage the individual on a fundamental bodily, spatial level, he unwittingly was describing Minimalism as a subjective art, that is, an art invoking the last sign of tragic subject, even according to Mondrian, as previously noted. Morris doesn't realize that "minimalist" engagement articulates the vanishing subject, bespeaks, as Adorno remarks, the most paradoxically essential reality of today's world: the subject in the act of vanishing. Morris shows it holding on for dear life as it is being deconstructed into spatial terms (today these would be sociolinguistic). It is this "holding on" which characterizes the minimalist will to art, especially the minimalist line. Its maximal implication—form—is this subjective "holding on."

The minimalist act of art is as attenuated an act of art as it is possible to make; it is certainly a long way from Clyfford Still's absolute Act. Yet like that Act the minimalist act of art bespeaks an insecure yet defiant subjectivity. I take this obsession with making fundamental acts of art to be the increasingly obvious central problematic of modern art, in large part unconsciously responsible for the proliferation of modern styles ("experimentalism")—the repeated deterioration and renewing of the act of art, the preoccupation with the novel act of art even when the idea of novelty has become bankrupt. This proliferation may even one day be regarded as more a sign of insecure selfhood than of the optimistic "modern" belief in mastery of material and form, emulating the extraordinary fertility of technological invention. Modern art is left increasingly with a goalless, "technical" act—all the more transparent subjectively because of its goallessness. Minimalism is the final state of abandonment of art to this subtle modern goallessness, the snake in the bosom of modern abundance of styles. Art is doomed, Sisyphus-like, to repeat its act—which is exactly the condition of modern subjectivity seeking to escape administration, control of the System. There is important—fundamental—existential meaning in art's reduction to the Sisyphean—minimalist—state.

Minimalism bespeaks the same awareness of the self-conscious, problematic—and peculiarly defensive as well as offensive—character of the act of art that Duchamp had. Duchamp shows the act of art in an already involuted, crippled state when he reduces it to a matter-of-fact intention, whose results are not only far from clear and inherently uncertain in meaning, but simply don't matter. The irony of the Duchampian act of "artistic" choice is reflected in the banality—triviality—of the object chosen, anointed as "art"; but it is an irony which shows the absurdity of the choice—of the act of "art." André Breton regarded Duchamp's readymades as "manufactured objects promoted to the dignity of works of art through the choice of the artist."[20] Again, there is by implication a struggle with the machine—and submission to it by "choosing" one of its products. The choice—"art" reduced to an obvious act—conveyed by the artist's signature which "sweeps briefly over the narrowly defined object . . . and then focuses upon a whole mental process," is not only more important for its self-consciousness than it is for its "artistic" results, but that self-consciousness is the "artistic" result, the real "object" of art. As Breton wrote, the actual object has become "increasingly self-denying" stripped of "its anecdotic and accidental elements so that it would finally appear 'as itself,' after eternity had wrought its final changes in it."[21] This is the same eternity that purifies Mondrian's color-planes and intensifies his lines, that gives his aesthetic plastic "abstract-real life."[22] But the "artistic" choice—act of "art"—that set this eternity in motion, a choice which Breton characterizes as the consequence of a "policy of absolute negation,"[23] and which is as much Mondrian's as Duchamp's policy, is where the entire effort to eliminate the spontaneously and naturally tragic began—and where the futility of the effort was acknowledged by the very determination with which the goal was pursued.

The question is, why was the effort to transcend the tragic made in the first place? What had happened to the act of art that made it want to purify itself of the dualistic life-world, in part by becoming a "meaningless" choice? What was Duchamp's "mental process" in making the choice? What in the modern period led to this push to minimize the tragic in art which seems to have culminated in Minimalism—and yet only returns it in a more intractable, irreducible way? What led to the paradoxical result of the act of art becoming insecure, uncertain of any goal but itself, that is, wanting nothing but to be willed—not wanting to make anything in particular, but just to be made, as proof that the entire enterprise of art-making is not futile? Even if it can never help humanity to harmony, even if it is socially useless, even if it only reflects the tragedy of being human—the act of art must be made, whatever its results. It is its own result. Minimalism shows the unexpected pathos in the Minimalist reflection of this tautological situation—the pursuit of self-identity in the face of all loss of identity in a world that has become too "modern" for its own good. The minimalist act of art paradoxically becomes an act of will resisting the modernity which has transferred all will to technology—and regards all acts as "technicalities" within the System.

It was the experience of modernity itself, the sense of being inexhaustibly present—the urgency of nowness, the compulsion to be everlastingly new, issuing in a sense of overwhelming presence—that is finally signalled by the minimalist line, which has no history. Indeed, it often appears "prehistoric." The systemic simplicity of minimalist presence created by the minimalist line epitomizes the paradox of being totally modern yet refusing the momentum—the mechanism—of modernism, as represented by the machine. In the minimalist line the mechanical aesthetic has at last spent itself without forfeiting the sense of the necessary nowness of art. But the minimalist line also lets us know this nowness is an invented fiction, a reluctant reality. Like all art it creates an illusion, the task of illusion being not to represent the world but to dominate it, suppress it, transcend it. The minimalist line does this while articulating the bankruptcy of the modern world which it seems to represent succinctly. In its paradoxical brevity and unity all the modern hopes for a transcendental art in a transcendental society are concentrated and crushed. The minimalist line represents the simultaneous frustration and fullness of modern oppositional intellectual art in a life-world that no longer wants elementary truths from art, forcing the elementary act of art back on itself. In the minimalist line absolute art implodes; all its zeal, once socially directed, is now directed to preserving a vestige of the idea of art. As Freud wrote, what is taken "to be a new life is a reflection of the past"; it is the same with new art. The minimalist line repeats within its Elementaristic form the paradigm of the avant-garde: to begin with a social mission, and to end in aesthetic novelty—to begin with a socially revolutionary intention and to end epitomizing the surprise of the new (the experience of "modernity") in its most radical form. Paradoxically, this turns out to be unexpectedly familiar, perceptually ordinary. It is as Hegel, in the *Phenomenology of Spirit,* said of the pure idea, spirit that has at last become absolute or pure in itself after concretizing through history: it dialectically converts into the banal "here and now." Its destiny fulfilled, it becomes merely typical.

In looking at the works in this exhibition, one recognizes what should ideally be distinguished as optimistic and pessimistic articulations of the line; but in almost every instance there is a paradoxical mix of intentions—unintended irony emerging from what is an intended method of contradiction. In what is for me the single most stunning—conceptually as well as perceptually—work, Gordon Matta-Clark hews a line out of a building (*Humphrey Street Splitting,* Englewood, New Jersey, 1974), in a devastating, apocalyptic act of art. It reverberates with meaning—it is a symbolic enactment of art's revenge on an indifferent society—but it ends as a pure act of art. A banal social product—a commonplace American house—is destroyed by a strong will to artistic power: the individual artist's will goes against the social will embodied in the manufactured house, destroys it, but implicitly accomplishes nothing but "making art"; there are many more houses where the destroyed one came from. Indeed, it was about to be destroyed anyway, to be replaced by the latest—typically new—house. The split is a statement of individuality in the face of anonymity—an absolute act in a contingent world—but the individuality takes the form of a geometrical platitude. In the end, it is the act as such that matters—the human will embodied in it—not whether it is an act of art or social act, produces absolute art or has social revolutionary (anarchistic?) implications, or both. The genius of Matta-Clark is to have forced us to recognize both the act of art and the social act which produced the house as acts of human will—of the will to power. The futility of both acts is implicit, as well as the absurdity of the will to power, which exists more for itself than to effect anything stupendously significant. Matta-Clark's split is an extraordinarily profound, climactic work of absolute art, showing both it and the life-world it was meant for dead-ended in ironic acts, which neither intended to be ironic. Their irony explores them as acts, making them signs of metaphysically nihilistic will.

Walter de Maria's *Las Vegas Piece* (1969), Dennis Oppenheim's *Boundary Split* and *Timc Line* (both 1968), and the proposed but never executed *Dream Lines* (1976), all reminiscent of the lines of Nazca Robert Morris wrote about (if different in material), hew a line out of nature much as Matta-Clark hewed one out of society. But the effect is not the same because the result is less destructive. A mark, a gesture—an implicitly commemorative sign—reminds us that nature is the only immortality, calls attention to the durability of the context of the transient line, particularly in Oppenheim's case. Time is the implicit—in Oppenheim, explicit—subject matter; not even the pyramids will last forever, and even de Maria's cuts will crumble, and come increasingly to resemble the natural ruts of erosion in the earth. He is quite conscious of this, and the lines can be said to meditate on it. Indeed, the meditative—pensive—quality of the lines in all cases again shows what happens to the absolute act of art when it is carried to an extreme in a non-art context: it recalls forces greater than art, or the individual will that made the primary act of art. The more urgently physical the act of art the more metaphysical its implications—the more it transcends the conditions of its making to make a point about the power of "absolute" art to signify absolute sources of power. Art abandons—leapfrogs over—the society that has abandoned it; no longer believing that it can change daily existence, art communes with the ground of being.

Cecile Abish's *Cut Line* (1971) is the *dernier cri* of the mechanical aesthetic, a perverse demonstration of the fraudulent, abortive alliance of absolute art and the machine. A machine that cuts a line and a line that is a machine—or is it the machine that is the cut line?—brings to the fore the unexpectedly Kafkaesque dimension of the mechanical aesthetic: the sense of absolute art's claustrophobic containment within the mechanical, and of the new claustrophobia—more politely called hermeticism—of absolute art. But in *At Eighths and Sixteenth's* (1972) the vanishing perspective, a perverse response to the architectural context, reminds us that the Minimalists have always sought to break the stranglehold of this hermeticism by locating absolute art in, or rather deriving it from, a life-world situation, transcending preconceptions of social reality. The self-contradictory situational character of much Minimalist work in general reminds us of the fundamental ambiguity of its intention, an ambiguity that is not simply the result—or acknowledgement—of the inevitable language-game that modern art seems to reduce to, but rather that the Minimalist act of art begins and ends in the life-world. The Minimalist act is not simply a "comment" on it, but a demonstration that, because it can be subject to an "artistic" intervention, the life-world has more implications than are evident from the status quo of its appearances. The self-evidence—self-evident here-and-nowness—of the Minimalist act of art is designed to be a critical intervention in the superficial self-evidence of the life-world, disrupting it to reveal its depth of meaning, the irony of its own apparent straightforwardness.

Christo's *Running Fence* (1972) grandly capsulates the Minimalist problematic: a transient, essentially simple, construction, intervenes in—contradicts—a context of nature and society, with complex results. Again, technology and absolute art are one, in the name of social harmony—a temporary oneness in a field of self-evidently absolute natural and social difference—in a condition of apparently insurmountable disharmony. But art shows this disorderly natural and especially social condition to be "unnecessary"—to lack "internal necessity." Only the absolute act of art which the fence represents has internal necessity; for all its transience, it reminds us of the eternal possibility of social harmony. The story of Christo's horrendous legal efforts to cross various properties—to build the fence in the first place—is as much a part of its structure as the actual method of construction and the variegated terrain it crosses (and "binds"). Minimalism demonstrates that absolute art is as much—if not more—constructive intention as "mechanical" physicality. It is through the reduction of art to pure act that meaning and structure fuse seamlessly, especially when that pure act is inseparable from a life-world.

Even Carl Andre's *Lever* (1969) is bound to the life-world—whatever its museum destiny—simply through its material (brick, in this case), which is also the case in Alan Shields's *Rope Painting* (1969–70) and Stephen Antonakos's *Incomplete Neon Square* (1974), and even Eleanor Antin's *100 Boots Facing the Sea* (1971). The intervention in these works is to dislocate a life-world material so that it acquires metaphysical import, signalling at once the primitive act of art and that act's power to disclose the power within the void. The Antin piece particularly, with its "environmental impact," demonstrates the power in the "straight" act, if with an almost self-defeating irony, for the boots are too directly evocative of the human figure, a presence distracting from the artistic and metaphysical "problems" implicit in the work. For all its social import—for all that it has to do with the status of human will in the modern world—the minimalist line is not "about" the human figure, not even as an indirect presence. For human presence reduces the act of art to its servant, which undermines its power of intervention and metaphysical disclosure.

The works by George Rickey, Nancy Holt, and Forest Myers reflect the mechanical aesthetic directly, for all their material and technological differences. (Myers creates a laser construction; I emphasize its "constructivist" aspect, which is also evident in Rickey and Holt.) Ellsworth Kelly's various lines concretize the idea of autonomous absolute art. Yet even in Kelly autonomy has mechanical, if not specifically rationalist, implications. His lines are completely beside the social point, which is finally why they lose whatever metaphysical impact they intended. Their purity shows how splendid a blind alley autonomy can be. In the works by Hans Haacke and Beverly Pepper the "act" of art, in my opinion, is almost completely subsumed by the material of the object, and its "functionality"—inadvertent in Pepper's case, deliberate in Haacke's. This doesn't deny the act's presence, but it makes it less of an Act; its metaphysical implications, if not denied, are submerged, and certainly undermined—beside the point—in Haacke's work. Yet taken "absolutely," Haacke's piece reveals the sublime impacted within the matter-of-fact manifestation of nature's workings. In Robert Grosvenor's work, the loss of the Act in the material also seems about to be enacted: the "art" seems to abide in the "enacted" material—the splintering broken wood, calling attention to its raw state at the point of breakage of the wood beam. Yet that act of breakage signals almost as raw a will as Matta-Clark's work. But it is not as sublime, for it is not constituted by the void as Matta-Clark's split is. It is Matta-Clark who has taken Barnett Newman's "zip" in the void—making the void itself a zip (Malevich's void became a non-objective feeling)—to its logical conclusion. Matta-Clark made the first authentically Minimalist line into an abyss of meaning.

1. Piet Mondrian, "From the Natural to the Abstract: From the Indeterminate to the Determinate" (1918), *De Stijl*, ed. Hans L. C. Jaffe (New York, Harry N. Abrams, 1971), p. 76.
2. Mondrian, pp. 76–77.
3. Mondrian, p. 77.
4. Ibid.
5. For an examination of art in the administered world see T. W. Adorno, *Aesthetic Theory* (London, Routledge & Kegan Paul, 1984).
6. Naum Gabo, "Sculpture: Carving and Construction in Space" (1937), *Theories of Modern Art*, ed. Herschel B. Chipp (Berkeley, University of California Press, 1968), p. 336.
7. Mondrian, p. 77.
8. Piet Mondrian, "A Dialogue on Neoplasticism" (1919), Hans L. C. Jaffe (New York, Harry N. Abrams, 1971), p. 120.
9. Theo van Doesburg, "The Will to Style (The New Form Expression of Life, Art and Technology)" (1922), in Joost Baljieu, *Theo van Doesburg* (New York, Macmillan Publishing Co., 1974), p. 122.
10. Kasimir Malevich, "Introduction to the Theory of the Additional Element in Painting" (1927), *Theories of Modern Art*, ed. Herschel B. Chipp (Berkeley, University of California Press, 1969), p. 338.
11. Malevich, p. 343.
12. Gabo, p. 336.
13. Piet Mondrian, "The Realization of Neoplasticism in the Distant Future and in Architecture Today" (1922), *De Stijl*, ed. Hans L. C. Jaffe (New York, Harry N. Abrams, 1971), p. 165.
14. Mondrian, p. 164.
15. Ibid.
16. Mondrian, "From the Natural to the Abstract: From the Indeterminate to the Determinate," p. 76.
17. Mondrian, "The Realization of Neoplasticism in the Distant Future and in Architecture Today," p. 164.
18. Mondrian, "From the Natural to the Abstract: From the Indeterminate to the Determinate," p. 76.
19. Ibid.
20. André Breton, "Marcel Duchamp" (1934), *Surrealism and Painting* (New York, Icon Editions, Harper & Row, 1972), p. 88.
21. André Breton, "Artistic Genesis and Perspective of Surrealism" (1941), *Surrealism and Painting* (New York, Icon Editions, Harper & Row, 1972), p. 72.
22. Mondrian, "From the Natural to the Abstract: From the Indeterminate to the Determinate," p. 78.
23. Breton, "Marcel Duchamp," p. 87.

Twenty Years of Purification
Phyllis Tuchman

Twenty years ago a wave of purification later known as Minimalism swept across the art world. A formal language of austerity coupled with arcane, intellectual content rapidly became the new period style. Raw emotions, nuanced surfaces, and spiky elements were replaced by serial systems, smooth planes, and trued edges. Bald, abstract structures and geometrically arrayed compositions toppled the hegemony of Abstract Expressionism and additionally challenged traditional notions of what constituted sculpture and painting.

Although its forms have always been straight forward, direct, even blunt, Minimalism itself hardly evolved simplistically. Any student of art history can name Carl Andre, Dan Flavin, Donald Judd, Sol LeWitt, and Robert Morris as the dominant figures who initiated the movement. And the exhibition considered to have signaled its presence is also familiar—*Primary Structures: Younger American and British Sculptors* organized by Kynaston McShine at the Jewish Museum in the Spring of 1966. But the latest manifestations as well as the brief period before the nature of Minimalism coalesced, are rarely acknowledged.

Minimalism indisputably transformed the practice of sculpture during the '60s and '70s. Process and procedure remain important components of its legacy to the art world. Unexpectedly, however, the term 'minimalism' has come to enjoy a life of its own. In recent years it has been appropriated by daily newspaper reporters and national news magazine writers to describe trends in music, dance, clothing, interior design, gourmet cooking, and even floral arrangements. Like Surrealism, Minimalism has been integrated into the general public's vocabulary to refer to instances independent of the context of painting and sculpture. In a manner comparable with the way someone might say an unlikely situation or an odd juxtaposition of objects is surreal, anything spare, terse, uncluttered might today evoke the use of Minimalism as an apt designation.

By 1966 it was clear that Minimalism's chief practitioners were artists working in three dimensions. Once this notion was grasped by critics and curators, its earliest phase was hardly ever mentioned again. Cool Art, The Third Stream, ABC Art, and Art of the Real, nevertheless, survive as the titles of articles and an exhibition which convey the more inclusive character of Minimalism early on.

At first the new sleek, rigorous, somewhat reductivist manner was associated with an art which was considered to be neither wholly pictorial nor wholly sculptural. By integrating properties or attributes from both sectors of the fine arts, it was reckoned that a new species of art was being achieved. Statements by one of Minimalism's most fervent champions and by one of its leading artists make this plain. In the Spring 1965 issue of *Art Voices* Lucy Lippard wrote. "The boundaries between traditionally understood media are becoming increasingly difficult to define with the advent of a group of young non-objective artists who are strongly denying the existence of any such boundaries." Soon afterwards, in *Arts Yearbook 8,* Donald Judd coolly asserted, "Half or more of the best new works in the last few years has been neither painting nor sculpture."

During the early '60s scores of paintings and sculptures were assuming new looks. It was not unusual to find that what was mounted against walls had bulging planes or else three-dimensional elements appended to otherwise pristine surfaces, and occasionally, canvas edges resembled geometry lessons. This type of work became categorized as shaped canvas and experienced a brief vogue. Pieces resting directly on the floor dispensed with the need for pedestals. They had applied color. Moreover, since they were constructed in wood, and later on fabricated in metals, they were neither carved, modelled, nor welded. This breed of object gave rise to Minimalism and consequently proved to have great staying power. Today it is obvious that it was no accident that four of the five principal Minimalists began their careers as painters. Once Flavin, Judd, LeWitt, and Morris translated the concerns with which they had dealt in their canvases into three dimensions, their art became more forceful, convincing, and immediate.

The meteoric ascent of Minimalism throughout the Western world, always worthy of note, was particularly unusual. Art magazines, including *Artforum, Art International, Art in America, Arts, Art News, Arts Yearbook,* and others, were constantly filled with illustrations, articles, interviews, reviews, symposium responses, and advertisements concerning individual and collective endeavors. Readers were, in fact, told what to think about the new art before they had even had much of a chance to see the work for themselves. Minimalism was a *fait accompli* in the press by the time the art-going public was presented with a plethora of exhibitions. Galleries in New York, as well as across the country and in Europe, mounted one-person shows. Museums, which were devoting space to avant-garde tendencies with greater frequency than in the past, also generated much attention.

Minimalism's exhibition history was especially instrumental in its rise from obscurity to the forefront of art activities in the space of a few short years. In just four art seasons the new art progressed from a small group show in a Manhattan gallery, to an ambitious display of three-dimensional art in a New York museum, to a sprawling survey in a West Coast museum, to the prestige of a major installation organized by a European institution.

During January 1965 *Shape and Structure,* a group show on view in the former East 72nd Street brownstone quarters of the Tibor de Nagy Gallery, directed by John Bernard Myers, offered the public its first extended sampling of Minimalism. Organizers Henry Geldzahler, Barbara Rose, and Frank Stella, who were then all in their twenties, selected ten artists who were mostly new on the scene: sculptors Carl Andre, Donald Judd, Robert Morris, and Robert Murray and painters Walter Darby Bannard, Larry Bell, Charles Hinman, Will Insley, Neil Williams, and Larry Zox. A fresh, optimistic tone prevailed. Instead of confronting the kind of emotional displays and slapdash pyrotechnics associated with the 10th Street touch of the previous generation, viewers were greeted by cheerful colors, forthright images, and the sureness of geometry. The title for the show, determined only after the participants were selected, underscored how, regardless of media and individual pursuits, all ten sculptors and painters were dealing with "a characteristic visible form" as well as "the interrelation of parts as dominated by the general character of the whole." Nevertheless, in a review in *Art News,* critic Kim Levin raised an interesting issue which has never been resolved in the literature on Minimalism. She wrote, "Almost any one of the artists' work seen separately gives an impression of severity and hardness, but together turned out to be surprisingly zany, decorative and vivid. . . ."

Fifteen months later the fifty-one works Kynaston McShine included in the *Primary Structures* exhibition at the Jewish Museum provided an in-depth focus on what had previously been referred to as post-geometric structures, object sculpture, and specific objects. General characteristics could be discerned: an aura of accomplishment surrounded the art and generated a great deal of serious criticism. Today, perusing a list of participating artists, one discovers a variety of Minimalists and non-Minimalists who have subsequently dominated the international sculpture scene for much of the past two decades: Carl Andre, Richard Artschwager, Larry Bell, Ronald Bladen, Anthony Caro, Walter De Maria, Dan Flavin, Robert Grosvenor, Donald Judd, Ellsworth Kelly, Sol LeWitt, John McCracken, Robert Morris, Forrest Myers, Tim Scott, Tony Smith, Robert Smithson, Anne Truitt, William Tucker, and Isaac Witkin. A few of the artists were then in their twenties; more than half had been born during the nineteen thirties. Several sculptors had never held one-person shows; those who had, had, for the most part, only presented one or two solo exhibitions. Age and experience were not handicaps, however: much that was on view came to alter the face of American art.

What was startlingly original also looked astonishingly simple. Smooth surfaces, crisp edges, and monochromatic planes predominated. Occasionally the art was cumbersome and bulky. There were no pedestals in sight; nothing had been cast in bronze. Everything was wholly abstract. Much was lushly colored. Several multipart sculptures consisted of elements separated by spatial intervals. There were pieces installed on walls; two hung from the ceiling; another spanned a corner. A good deal of imagery was generated by serial systems and other logically-directed programs. In 1966 the materials employed were unorthodox: firebrick, formica, fiberglass, fluorescent light, latex, linoleum, masonite, painted canvas, plexiglass, painted aluminum, baked enamel, chrome plate, galvanized iron, chrome, brass, plastic, and polyester resin.

The viewer was not meant merely to respond directly to the language of form, but also to reflect upon a host of intellectual issues suggested by the language. Interpretations could be gleaned from sources not previously associated with the appreciation of art. Philosophical discourse, psychological theories, and mathematical reasoning provided keys to understanding what had been made in three dimensions. Coming to grips with primary structures is less a matter of connoisseurship and more one of ideation. Unlike the direct-metal sculptors of the previous decade who had been profoundly affected by the animated word play of James Joyce's *Ulysses,* the younger artists represented a generation more readily predisposed to being enthralled by *A Skeleton Key to Finnegan's Wake.* The former involves immediate experience and a regard for the properties of fiction; the latter is more engaged with explication and analysis.

Relying upon fabricators and preformed modules was a further assertion that art was about ideas, not craft. Although several artists who participated in *Primary Structures* executed their own pieces, Hilton Kramer insightfully mentioned in a review of the show in the *New York Times* that "the sculptural imagery they aspire to does not require them to do so." He further noted, "Fundamental to this new aesthetic is an attitude of detachment and impersonality—an attitude that finds its proper expression in forms and materials that do not require the intervention of the artist's hand. . . ."

McShine presented primary structures as sculpture related to but quite distinct from painting. In his matter-of-fact introduction he described how painting had recently been transformed. Now he argued it was possible to see how sculptors were comparably reassessing their craft. Questions were being raised about the use of pedestals; the way sculpture, space, and spectator interacted; and the selection of materials. While artists dealing with three dimensions were influenced by painting as well as twentieth-century engineering and architecture, as McShine saw it, many sculptors were even more "critical and radical." In addition, their art was "more philosophical and conceptual in content." According to McShine, by dominating environments with large scale and architectural proportions, immense indoor works "carried an implicit social criticism."

Hilton Kramer's observation in 1966 that "a new aesthetic era is upon us" was particularly clear a year later when the Los Angeles County Museum of Art sponsored *American Sculpture of the Sixties,* curated by Maurice Tuchman. The 166 works, installed indoors as well as outside, were executed by eighty artists active on both coasts. Besides Minimalist structures, there were examples of welded-metal construction, funk art, tableau-like scenes, environmental work, and Pop. Although most of the pieces by Andre, Flavin, Judd, LeWitt, and Morris as well as those by Ronald Bladen, Walter De Maria, John McCracken, and Tony Smith, who can be considered para-Minimalists, had been exhibited previously, it did not matter. McShine had wanted to show new art—and some sculptures he put on view were so new, they were not reproduced in the catalogue—but Tuchman was producing a context. The very nature of his institution, a museum which displayed paintings and sculptures from various cultures, made it possible to tender credentials to avant-garde tendencies in an old master setting. And Minimalism emerged with high marks. An unassailable confidence, an identifiable sensibility, and an adventuresome range of concerns among its practitioners could not be denied. Moreover, the Minimalist enterprise dominated attention in an exhibition that, more than any other, asserted that sculpture had finally come of age in the United States a decade after American or, more specifically, Abstract Expressionist painting had achieved world renown. Minimalism earned for three-dimensional art in this country new respect and influence.

The publication Tuchman edited also deserves mention. It was one of the first megacatalogues to be issued by a museum. Today it is more of a reference book than the record of a show. In addition to color and black and white illustrations, artists' statements, biographies and bibliographies, it contains essays by ten critics, including Clement Greenberg and Barbara Rose. By critically reviewing all types of sculpture made since World War II, the catalogue contributed further to the feeling that what was on view in the museum was of paramount significance.

Critical articles, historical overviews, and artists' commentaries appeared in a special summer issue of *Artforum* devoted to American sculpture and published in conjunction with the show at the Los Angeles County Museum of Art. A lively dialogue on three-dimensional art was being spread across the country. And "Art and Objecthood," Michael Fried's fiery critique of the failure of what he termed literal (*viz.* Minimalist) art in the June 1967 *Artforum* was probably the most controversial essay on art to be published during the sixties. The article was serious, closely-argued, philosophical, and studded with a battery of footnotes and italicized words, phrases, and even whole sentences. In *Marsyas 15,* a publication of New York University's Institute of Fine Arts, Melissa McQuillan analysed her former professor's style: "Beginning with a descriptive statement of fact, [Fried] slips into a statement of personal perception, then to a passage in which he speaks for the spectator in general, from there to a kind of heightened personal perception, once more to a role of spokesman for the spectator, and from there to an impassioned metaphysical conception, hardly changing tone; if one follows and agrees with the perceptions, one is tempted to accept the metaphysics, not for what it is but also as a statement of fact."

Fried maintained that literalist art deserved a place in the history of sensibility rather than the history of taste. He believed that the concerns of literalist artists were not the same as those which engaged Modernist painters and sculptors. For example, according to Fried, attitudes towards shape were fundamentally different. A Modernist painter wanted shape to function pictorially rather than literally while a Minimalist sculptor "aspires, not to defeat or suspend its objecthood, but on the contrary to discover and project objecthood as such." Literalist art, he concluded, is antithetical to art because "objecthood amounts to nothing more than a plea for a new genre of theater; and theater is now the negation of art." By altering the relationship between the beholder and the sculpture, the literalist ultimately made it possible for the experience of the art to become more important than the quality of the art being experienced. "A kind of *stage* presence" was offered, a strategy far removed from "the modernist arts [where] nothing short of *conviction* . . . matters at all."

Fried's article relates to other Minimalist criticism

the way he contrasted Modernism with literalist art. He applied standards and criteria he believed all art should embody to Minimalism. Unlike previous critics who had avoided judgmental statements, Fried assumed a critical position. Others had noted that Minimalists had sought a new relationship between spectator and sculpture, but had left unsaid whether this occurrence was good or bad. Fried's "Art and Objecthood" is a chilling reminder that issues of quality should be treated before history neutralizes such matters.

During the 1967–68 art season another large museum exhibition cemented the latest stage in the spread of Minimalism. By then an international, not just an American, audience was being reached. The number of one-person shows held throughout the United States as well as in West Germany, France, Italy, the Netherlands, and Belgium were transforming artists' biographies into travel itineraries. *Minimal Art,* organized by Enno Develing with assistance from Lucy Lippard, opened at the Gemeentemuseum in The Hague on March 23, 1968. The participating artists were Andre, Bladen, Flavin, Robert Grosvenor, Judd, LeWitt, Morris, Tony Smith, Robert Smithson, and Michael Steiner. And just as *Artforum* had edited an issue to coincide with the sculpture show at the Los Angeles County Museum of Art, *Studio International,* then the leading English art journal, was belatedly inspired by the Dutch exhibition to publish features dealing with Minimalism by and about its practioners in its April 1969 edition.

The Hague's *Minimal Art* show was not just noteworthy because it took place on foreign soil. Besides importing American sculpture abroad, Develing injected a continental point of view into the proceedings. Indeed, the bilingual catalogue was geared more to the word than the object. Today what was on view cannot be reconstructed. There is simply no account of which five works by each of the ten artists were exhibited. Texts, not illustrations, fill the Gemeentemuseum's publication.

Develing's comments on Minimalism prefigure critical perspectives which would soon pervade interpretive material of the seventies. He wrote, "Here we have a reduction of forms to a primary state, often related to basic structures in geology, physics and chemistry, which do not so much reveal a state of mind, but rather a philosophy or ideology." Then Develing claimed, "Minimal art actually has little to do with art in a traditional sense, but more with our rapidly changing world and with the future of our society as suggested by the extremely important developments in science and technology."

Lucy Lippard abandoned the essay form of traditional criticism in "10 Structuralists in 20 Paragraphs," her contribution to the catalogue. With her prose she tried to parallel the style of the art objects under review. Her text nevertheless was typical of Minimalist criticism. Like many others, she stated her views, liberally quoted artists, mentioned how many Minimalists had begun their careers as painters and subsequently ignored sculptural precedents, suggested that Minimalism was unrelated and more progressive than the art championed by Clement Greenberg and Michael Fried, and peppered her remarks with allusions to various theoreticians outside the field of art. Still she made an interesting case for her assertion that, "There is more advanced sculpture than painting in America today." She noted that "sculpture, or in some cases a three-dimensional anti-sculpture, or structure, has provided an escape for those who feel the limitations of a pictorial idiom and an illusory surface are too great to be overcome."

At this juncture other exhibitions, catalogues, articles, and reviews continued to keep Minimalism before the public. And today, Andre, Flavin, Judd, LeWitt, and Morris are still active and continue to generate discussion. Even though art movements are generally short-lived, Minimalism has proved to have great staying power. Furthermore, it stands apart from other twentieth century art movements because its principal figures were not the only contributors to the wealth of ideas it encompassed. Although one can speak of satellite Cubists or minor Surrealists, the issues and practices which such para-Minimalists as Bladen, De Maria, McCracken, and Smith contributed cannot be belittled. The role of these four men in the total fabric of Minimalism has not been adequately investigated yet.

The lineage of Minimalism also merits further study. Painters inspired its early direction. The art of Barnett Newman, Frank Stella, Ellsworth Kelly, and Kenneth Noland looms large in Minimalism's first phases. Its primary state was sculptural, but during the seventies, its influence was felt in other cases. To be sure, Earthworks, a species of the plastic arts, brought Minimalism outside the confines of galleries and increased its scale tenfold. Yet, its impact was apparent as well in the kind of draftspersonship practiced by Mel Bochner, Dorothea Rockburne, and Richard Serra on exhibition walls. Photodocumentation owes a debt to Minimalism, too.

In all its manifestations, Minimalism has shown that form and content were not as inextricably wed to one another as it seemed to be in its purest three-dimensional condition. Early on, form was more crucial to its genesis. Later on, its philosophical and psychological content became more overpowering concerns. In whatever manner its forms and content have been synthesized, Minimalism has emerged as an enduring strain in the history of American art.

Reproductions and Statements

What is the role of the line *in your work of art in this exhibition?*

I chose a straight copper tube, because it seemed to be the easiest and cheapest way to cool an exposed surface with a refrigeration unit. Surfaces cooled to below freezing temperatures attract moisture from their surroundings and turn it into ice. It was the physical *interaction* between an object and its environment that interested me, not the shape of the object.

What is the relationship between the work in this exhibition and your subsequent work?

In preceding as much as in subsequent works, the interaction and interdependence of numerous elements, be they of a physical, biological or, later, a social nature, have been the focus of my work. I understood them, at the time, as examples of "realtime systems". I have since become wary of this term, because it has invited various misunderstandings. I also think that, like other seemingly exotic terms, it is easily fetishized and can be used to intimidate the uninitiated.

Ice Stick, 1966. Refrigeration unit, stainless steel, housing; 24 × 24 × 70". Lent courtesy Art Gallery of Ontario.

Geoffrey Clements

Untitled, 1975. Wood-creosote; 8′6″ × 8″ × 9″. Lent courtesy Paula Cooper Gallery, NYC.

What is the role of the line *in your work of art in this exhibition?*

The line in my fiberglass piece is drawn in a three-dimensional material although the work is basically two dimensional and painterly in nature. Visible is the action of pleating and fastening, part of a "process piece." It has both graphic and emotive elements.

What is the relationship between the work in this exhibition and your subsequent work?

Presently I've been working in a more three-dimensional mode. The pieces have drawn elements which are also expressive in nature, but the line is no longer rooted to a ground. The line comes from modeling, not process.

Fiberglass Wall Piece, **1973. Flannel soaked in polyester resin; 39½ × 25 × 2″. Lent courtesy Leo Castelli Gallery, NYC.**

Las Vegas Piece, 1969. Desert Valley (95 miles NE Las Vegas, Nevada). Photograph; 16 × 13½ × 1″. Lent courtesy the artist.

Two one-mile lines NS & EW perpendicular to each other and meeting at the N-W ends. The NS line is intersected at the half-mile point by a perpendicular half-mile line, directional EW. The EW mile line is intersected at the half-mile point by a perpendicular half-mile line, directional NS. The two half-mile lines meet at the SE point. The lines are 8-feet wide cuts in the earth. Curve lines are natural arroyo river markings.

Now I, 1965. Acrylic on canvas; 78 × 12". Lent courtesy Gerald S. Elliott.

What is the role of the line *in your work of art in this exhibition?*

The line is simply a vehicle for extending color and form into space. I used the line (as I had five years earlier in my "Minimal" paintings) to eliminate formal relationships within the work. (I felt that the compositional juggling of colors and shapes had reached a dead end.) The line made it possible for me to focus instead on a chosen color and material; its size and scale as it related to the viewer (both kinesthetically and in terms of his visual peception); and what happened to the line in actual physical space in terms of atmospheric perspective, reflected light, and its landscape setting.

What is the relationship between the work in this exhibition and your subsequent work?

"William Rush" was my first piece of sculpture. My second sculpture, "Stephen Long" (1968)—also a "line"—extended the three primary colors for 1600 feet (beyond the field of vision) and changed radically with fluctuating light and weather conditions. What had begun as a quest for "purity" and an interest in physical space was turning into a dialogue with the profuse phenomena of nature. By 1969 I had become interested in the color, texture, and moods of various natural environments, and the following year began building a continuous line-sculpture, now several miles long, in the woods of upstate New York ("Cyrus Field"). The line made it possible to preserve each natural site and ecology in toto, yet the experience of nature was restructured, related to human scale, and presented as art. Recently my work has tended toward large-scale environmental projects (architectural and urban; private landscapes and parks)—often based on natural forms—but I still use the line (disguised as paths, benches, walls, and bridges) to interweave and connect diverse elements, and to make the physical space manifest.

***William Rush,* 1966. Steel painted with red lead; 8 × 200 × ¼". Lent courtesy the artist.**

Untitled (Ice Piece), 1969. Fiberglass and wire; 744 × 1″. Lent courtesy Xavier Fourcade, Inc.

Lawrence Weiner

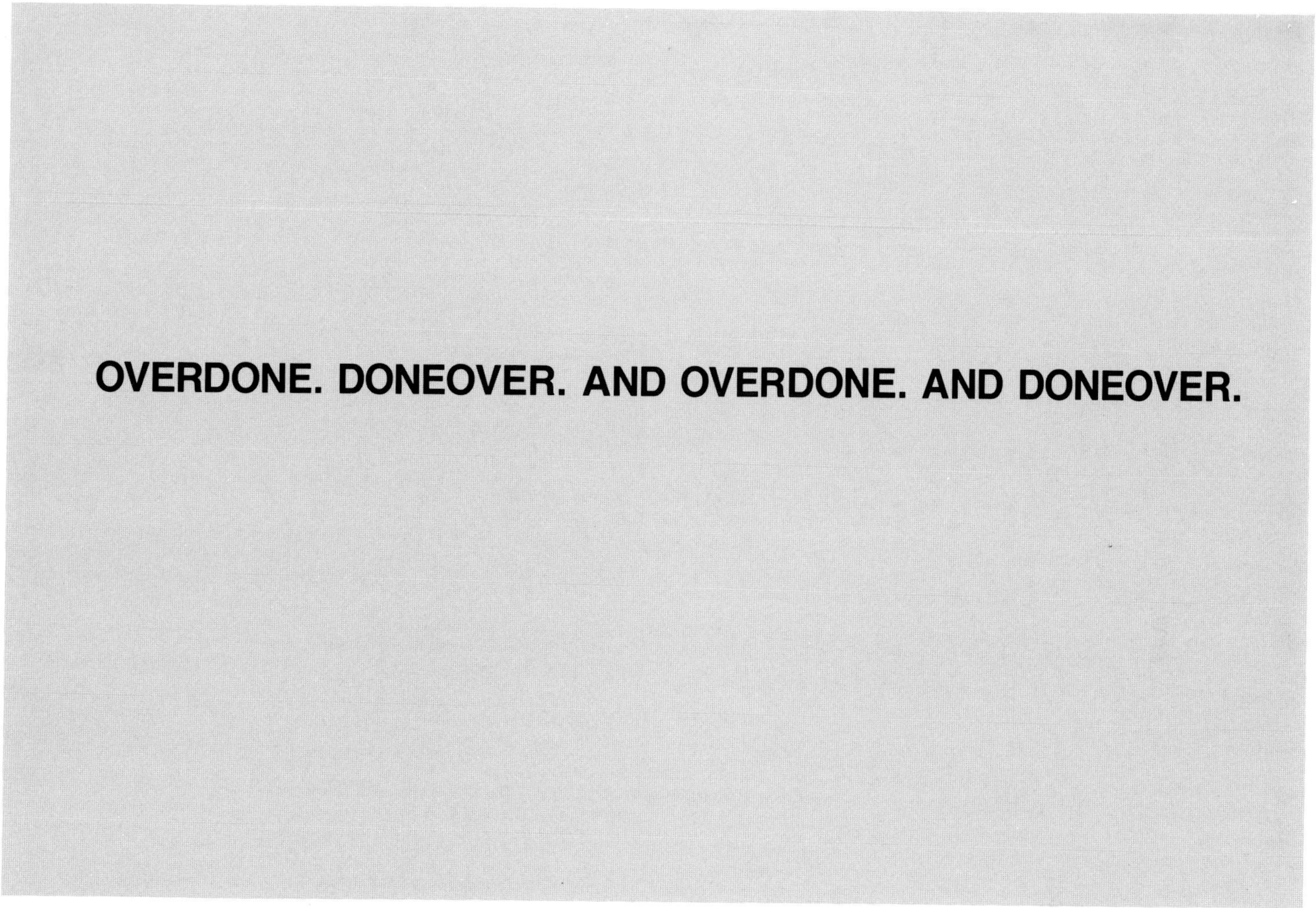

Overdone. Doneover. And Overdone. And Doneover., 1970. Language plus the material referred to. Lent courtesy Leo Castelli Gallery, NYC.

What is the role of the line *in your work of art in this exhibition?*

The line itself within the context of the work itself as a material reality.

What is the relationship between the work in this exhibition and your subsequent work?

The continuation of the research into and the presentation of the relationship of human beings to objects and objects to objects in relation to human beings.

Lima, c. 1966. Steel painted red, 7½ × 91 × 13". Lent courtesy Cintra Murray.

Although it is only a study for a much larger work, LIMA is typical of a group of pieces I did during the mid-sixties which were formed by cutting or burning almost all the way across a strip of metal plate—and by heating the remaining web, the freed planes could be tilted into casual relationhips. This method of working allowed me to achieve subtle shifts and changes of direction without destroying the unity of a single piece of metal.

In this particular piece my intention was to float a self-supporting horizontal plane—a thin red line, aproximately chest high. The size of the work would force viewers to contend with the sculpture in a physical sense, rather than simply look at it: an idea that must be credited to Barnett Newman.

A number of construction techniques were considered, such as honeycomb structured panels or parallel plates of prestressed aluminum or steel, held together by a series of "stand-offs."

Most of my sculpture from this period tended to be vertical and somewhat geometric in that it retained the flat, rectilinear qualities of steel or aluminum plate.

Floating Red Line, **1969. Wood; 24 × 24" × 20′. Not in exhibition.**

What is the role of the line *in your work of art in this exhibition?*

A vertical line or column as an expression of height, ascension, tree, ladder, stake, mast, megalithic stone, menhir, spine, tunnel, locus mundi. *A red line* suggesting blood, wounds, fire, passion, fire engine, play wagon and toy truck, celebration, church pomp and circus glitter. A *floating red line* incorporating suspension, flight, transcendence, levitation and Blackstone's Indian Rope Illusion. Gaston Bachelard said, ". . . of all metaphors, only those pertaining to height, ascent, depth, descent and fall are axiomatic. Nothing can explain them but they explain everything."

What is the relationship between the work in this exhibition and your subsequent work?

The columnar line, red, and floating/flying continue to be among my primary enthusiasms.

Lay of the Land, 1969. Laying down on my side, in an open field; a camera aimed out, toward the open field: I'm holding the camera first at my head, then at my chest, then at my stomach, then at my knees, then at my feet— a photograph is snapped from each position. Five black and white photographs; 20 × 20″. Lent courtesy the artist and Michael Klein, Inc.

What is the role of the line *in your work of art in this exhibition?*

The general notion of picking a point and following a line toward it (choosing a scheme and living up to it, finding a situation and adapting to it). A line was drawn from "my person" to "the world" ("I" attend "it," follow "it," adjust to "it"—a world considered as if it's "out there"). *Lay of the Land* considers my body as a line parallel to the line of the environment (the environment as panorama, as cinemascope movie screen); from each major point of my body, then, it's as if a line is drawn to each point on the landscape (the camera gives my body eyes); the landscape is "brought into line" of my body, the landscape is my body's landscape. *In Following Piece,* I make a bee-line for the person I've chosen to follow, but the piece finally turns back on me, the piece puts me in line: I become a passive receiver of another person's activity—once the initial scheme is decided upon, I have no mind of my own and blend into the crowd (it's as if I'm on a leash, dragged along by another person).

What is the relationship between the work in this exhibition and your subsequent work?

The early pieces set up "myself" as a starting point for my work: this "self" was something I could fall back on, something I could assume I knew at least something about, something that could be used as a source. In subsequent work, then, I could draw a line from that starting point out to other elements, other coordinates on a map of possible situations: from "I" to "him/her" (another agent), from "I" to "you" (the viewer), from "I" to particular cultures and histories (where the piece was installed). Eventually, this network of lines pulled me out of myself, and out of the work; the starting point had been therapeutic, had led to a follow-up, and now it wasn't necessary anymore.

There are some themes started in the early work that have continued up to the present: for example, the notion of being lost in space, blending into a landscape. Some recent architectural pieces have treated the dwelling as a human-like figure in which people using it might be lost, or swallowed up; this figure/dwelling, in turn, because of the materials it's made of, tends to seep into the environment it happens to be in.

Following Piece, 1969. Activity (street, people, pursuit). 23 days, varying durations New York City ("Street Works IV" Architectural League of New York). Lent courtesy the artist.

Betsy Jackson

Untitled (Orange Wall Relief), 1973. Fiberglass on wood; 93 × 21 × 4″. Lent courtesy Robert Elkon Gallery, Inc., NYC.

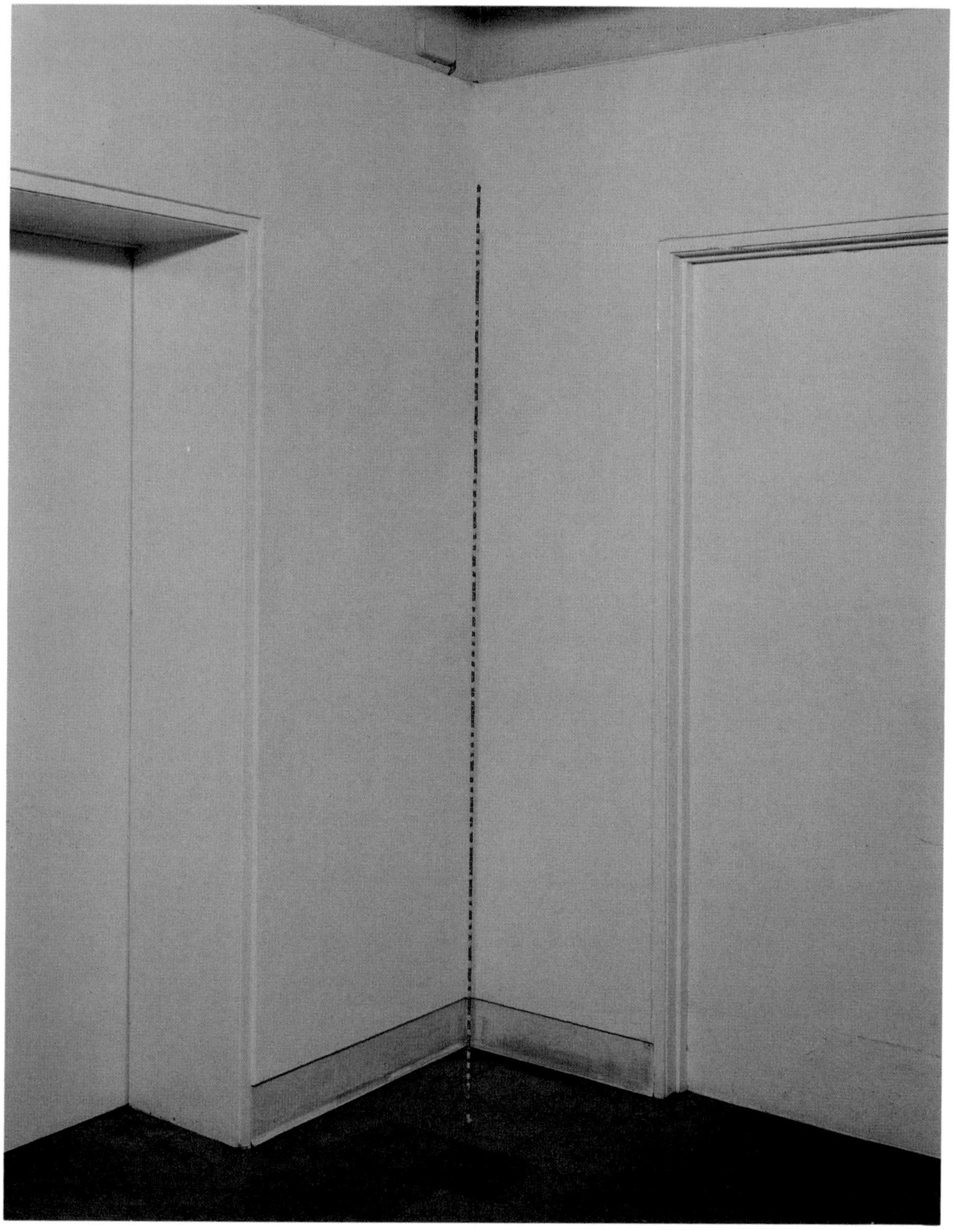

Eric Pollitzer

A) *Rope drawing (cornerpiece):* I was doing drawings of lines made up of as many dots (points) as could be separately distinguished; and also made up of a few dots that, however scanty, would still convey the idea and/or perception of a line. The rope drawing is made up of "dots" of liquitex, set standing 1/3 of its distance from the center of the corner, and lit by a spot (in line with it) that casts its shadow into the corner's seam, a single line thus yielded two lines of three planes (see drawing for installation).

B) *Meribah* (not shown): Meribah was the place where Moses struck the rock with his rod, and water gushed out. I wanted to make a word drawing that turned the place (Meribah) into a line (i.e. a rod). The word is stretched out to become an anamorph, that is, like the face at the text of Holbein's "Ambassadors," you can only read from the side. MERIBAH appears when you put your head against the left end of the line and squint along it. I've done—and still do—a lot of word-works. From 1969–70 I've done a great amount of work with dots (as line, as plane, as volume).

Untitled, **1973. Rope, liquitex, nylon; 87 × 3/8". Lent courtesy Charles Cowles Gallery.**

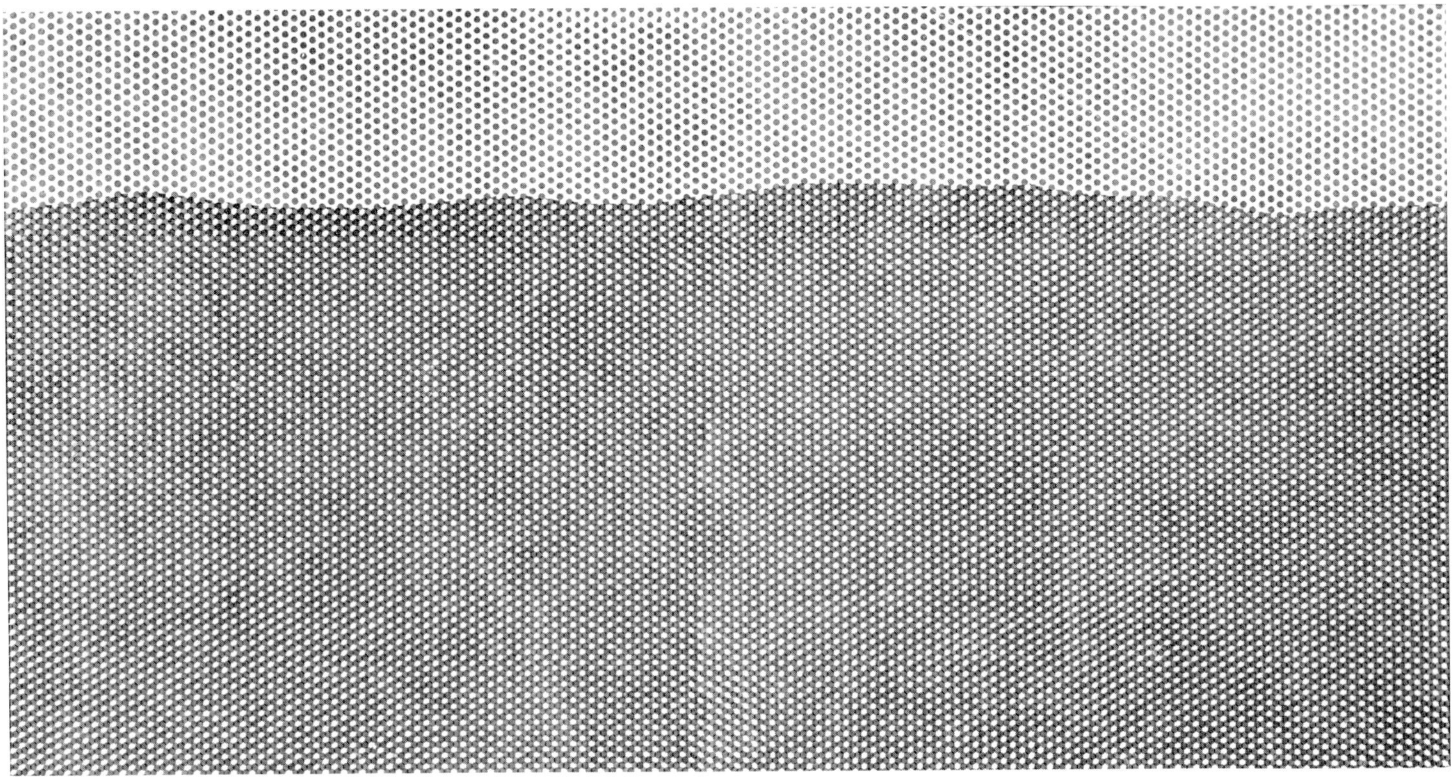

Blue Seascape, **1966. Oil and magna on canvas; 24 × 36″. Lent courtesy David Lichtenstein.**

What is the role of the line *in your work of art in this exhibition?*

The meaning of the line in this work is the sky.

What is the relationship between the work in this exhibition and your subsequent work?

I have redone the idea of sea and sky. The idea has remained basic, but the treatment of it has recurred in many different versions.

Eric Silverman

2" (2 inches), 1964–79. Each performance of this work, which Watts performed between 1964 and 1979, was done with this ribbon. Photograph during the Flux Fest at Fluxhall; "Street Events" on Canal Street, NYC, May 23, 1964. Ben Vautier and Allison Knowles and street traffic are seen performing the work. Photo documentation by George Maciunas. Lent courtesy The Gilbert and Lila Silverman Fluxus Collection.

What is the role of the line in your work of art in this exhibition?

The line in this instance is a ribbon that was cut as the opening piece in several Fluxus performances of events. Is that a line? Only Fluxus knows.

What is the relationship between the work in this exhibition and your subsequent work?

I doubt if there is a relationship. I recall it was an instantaneous idea to be used once.

Rite de Passage, 1971. Passage 1. Esplanade Avenue from the French Quarter to the statue of General Beauregard. A total distance of three miles. Photo documentation 30 × 40". Lent courtesy the artist.

For me, the laser is simply a tool that produces a line that is quite the most beautiful line that I have ever seen. This line has the potential to appeal to the viewer simply on the level of phenomena, like fireworks.

But the laser beam can introduce a kind of perspective into the architecture by moving into one's body space from a remote distance. It accumulates space as it moves, introducing a different sense of its dimensionality. In its last few hundred yards, it fills one's field of view as it passes over your space, communicating a totally different sense of scale than it has at its point of origin.

Solar Burn, Aries Day (Red), April 10, 1979 (remake of 1971–72 original). Sunlight, wood, and painted aluminum frame; 48½ × 16". Lent courtesy John Weber Gallery.

Walter Russell

Sunlight Convergence/Solar Burn Installation. Lent courtesy John Weber Gallery.

What is the role of the line *in your work of art in this exhibition?*

The sun draws a line by day. A focused point of light burns across a wooden plank. Each day the line is harvested and a solar narrative unfolds. A tale of weather and the motions of the earth. The line changes its curvature, reversing from winter to summer. It straightens ahead of time in the fall and behind time in the spring, before and after the equinoxes. Subtleties of earth speed and elliptical orbit are revealed in this energy portrait. End to end the daily curves form a double spiral similar to the spirals carved at New Grange and recently discovered in Chaco Canyon. An artwork drawn by rays of sunlight falling on the earth.

What is the relationship between the work in this exhibition and your subsequent work?

The Solar Burns brought dynamics of earth and sky directly into visible form. The sea of starlight that surrounds us became the subject matter of my art. Discoveries along the way led me to develop *Star Axis,* a large-scale earth/star work that has been under construction in New Mexico since 1976. *Star Axis* brings the motion of the stars to a personal measure so that we can feel the movement of the universe in relation to ourselves.

***Eight Unit Piece from Cayuga Salt Mine Project*, 1969. Mirrors and rock salt; 11 × 30 × 300″. Lent courtesy John Weber Gallery, NYC.**

This was the first interior underground site that I did, the one in the salt mine. There you have an amorphous room situation, an interior that's completely free. There's no right angles forming a rectilinear thing. So I'm adding the rectilinear focal point that sort of spills over into the fringes of the non-descript amorphousness. Then it's all contained when you shoot the photograph so you have that dialectic in that. On a topographical earth surface you don't have that kind of enclosure. There's a sort of rhythm between containment and scattering. It's a fundamental process that Anton Ehrenzweig has gone into. I think his views are very pertinent in that he talks about this in terms of containment or scattering.

An artist in a sense does not differentiate experience into objects. Everything is a field or maze, and you get that maze, serially, in the salt mine in that one goes from point to point. The seriality bifurcates: some paths go somewhere, some don't. You just follow and what you're left with is like a network or a series of points, and then these points can then be built in conceptual structures.

("Fragments of a Conversation," ed. William C. Lipke, in *The Writings of Robert Smithson,* NYU Press, 1979)

Humphrey Street Splitting, Englewood, New Jersey, 1974. Cibachrome photograph; 29¾ × 39½″. Lent courtesy Holly and Horace Solomon.

***A Line from the Lower Left Corner to the Upper Right Corner (No. 175),* 1973. Black crayon. Lent courtesy John Weber Gallery.**

Other works in the series:

165. A wall divided from corner to corner and side to side by a single broken line.

168. A line from the midpoint of the left side halfway toward the center of the wall.

169. A line from the midpoint of the left side to the center of the wall.

170. A line from the midpoint of the right side through the center of the wall toward the midpoint of the left side.

171. A line through the center of the wall toward the upper left corner, and a line from the center of the wall to the upper right corner.

174. A line from the midpoint of the left side to the upper right corner.

176. A horizontal line from the left side (more than half way, less than all the way).

177. A 48" (120 cm) horizontal line from the right side of the wall, 48" (120 cm) above the floor.

Nancy Anello

Line 10 Meters Long, 1959. Canister with label and fragment of a line, containing a black (ink) line on bluish paper; 8¾ × 393″. Lent courtesy The Gilbert and Lila Silverman Collection.

This year I was able to draw *A Line 7,200 Meters Long.* (The first series of lines, begun in the spring of 1959, had a maximum length of 33.63 meters.) This is the first of a series of exceptionally long lines of which I will leave one sample in each of the principal cities of the world. (Each line, when it is completed, will be vacuum-packed in a special stainless-steel case that will be hermetically sealed.) The series will be completed only when the sum of the lengths of the lines is equal to the circumference of the earth. (From *Zero #2,* "Immediate Projects")

Rotary Double Negative. 1969. Photograph: 2 × 12′. Lent courtesy Xavier Fourcade, Inc.

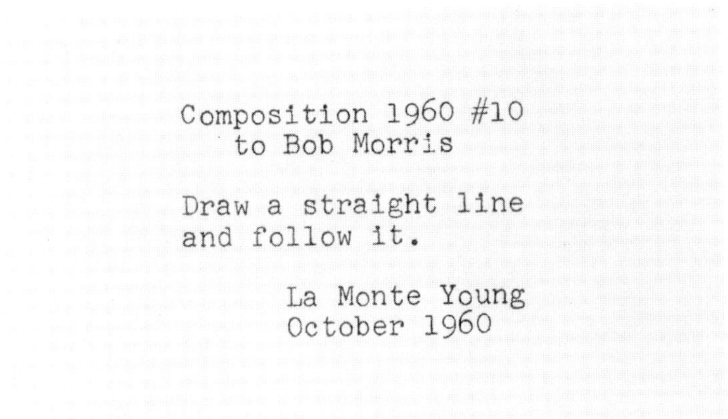
Composition 1960 #10
to Bob Morris

Draw a straight line
and follow it.

La Monte Young
October 1960

Composition 1960 #10, October 1960. 3⁷⁄₁₆ × 8½″. Lent courtesy the artist. © La Monte Young 1963

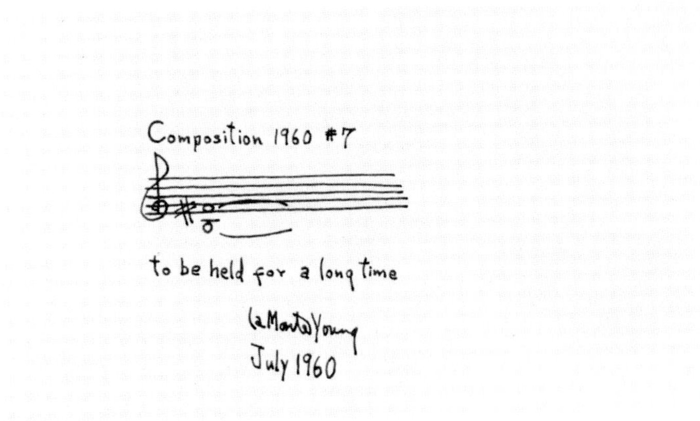

Composition 1960 #7, July 1960. Ink on paper; 3 × 5″. Lent courtesy the artist. © La Monte Young 1963

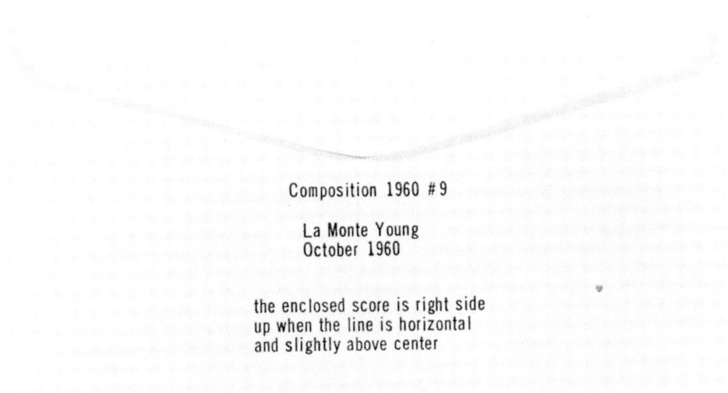

Composition 1960 #9, October 1960. Envelope; 3¾ × 6½″ envelope, 3 × 5″ card. Lent courtesy the artist.
© La Monte Young 1963

LY 1961, 1961. Book. Lent courtesy the artist.
© La Monte Young 1963

What is the role of the line *in your work of art in this exhibition?*

The realization of Composition 1960 #7 creates a straight line in sound.

In Composition 1960 #9 the line on the card is intended as a score to be interpreted by performers and was conceived as an answer to the graphic notations of John Cage.

In Composition 1960 #10 the line exists on many levels including the literal level of 'draw a straight line and follow it' as a performance work, and the metaphorical level in its relationship to life and art.

Using Composition 1960 #10 as an underlying structural constant, Compositions 1961 is a conceptual work in which I determined to compose my entire 1961 output in one linear stroke. Many of the works were performed before their date of composition.

What is the relationship between the work in this exhibition and your subsequent work?

Draw a straight line and follow it.

Marian Zazeela

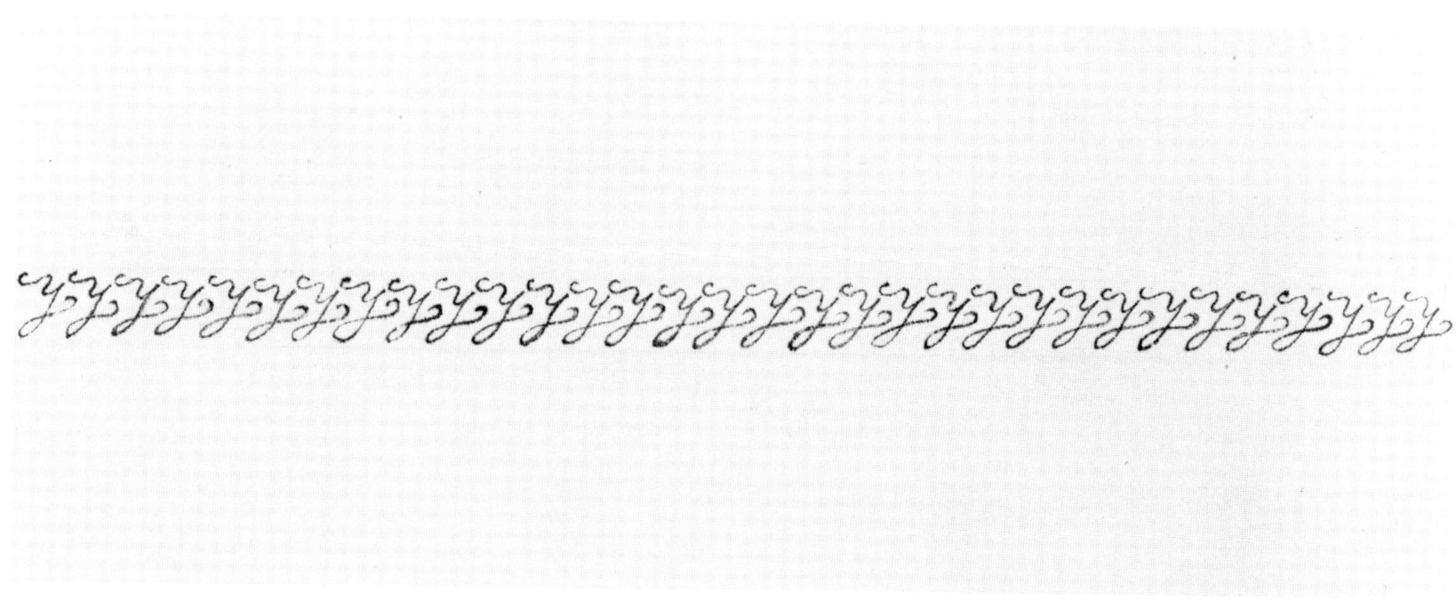

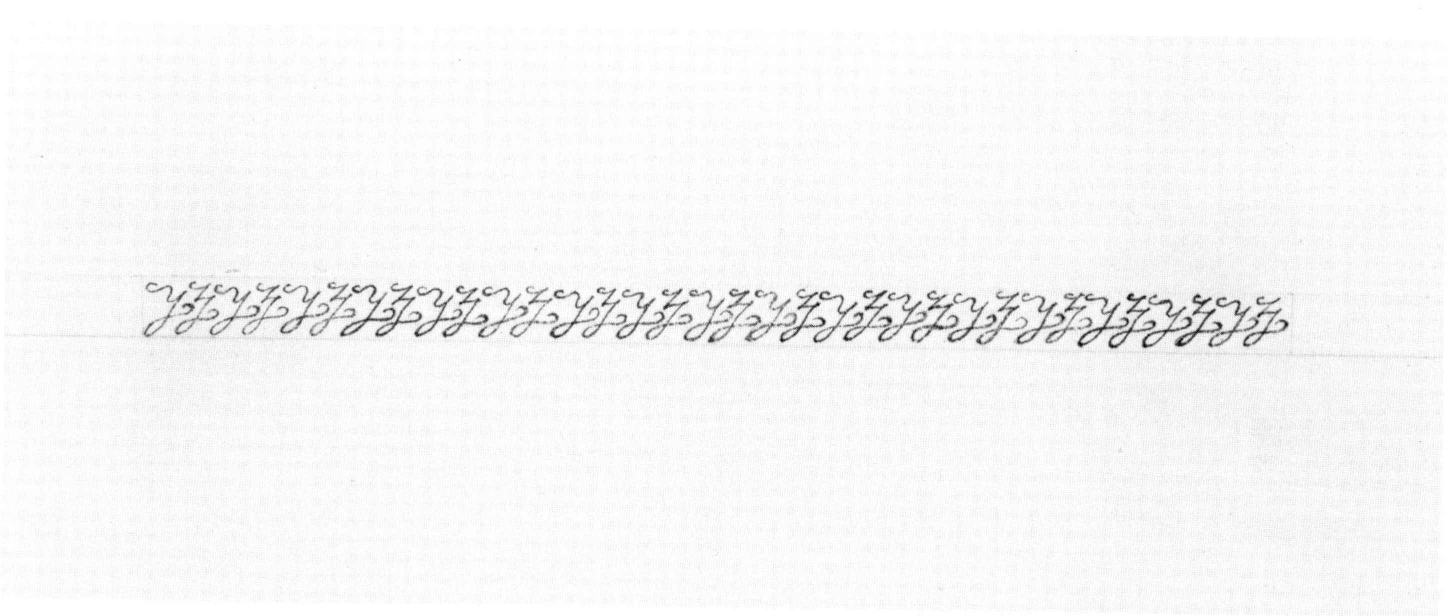

Line of Y's #1 **31364, 1964. India ink on rice paper; 7¾ × 10⅛" (image size) 9⁹⁄₁₆ × 13¹⁄₁₆" (paper size). Lent courtesy the artist.** © Marian Zazeela 1985

Line of Y's & Z's **31364, 1964. India ink on rice paper; 7¾ × 10" (image size) 9⅝ × 13 (paper size). Lent courtesy the artist.** © Marian Zazeela 1985

What is the role of the line *in your work of art in this exhibition?*

A line is a direct statement; it clarifies the issues by limiting the parameters under consideration.

These drawings are about looking at what appears to be a simple, straightforward line dividing a plane, and finding the intricate detail with which it is composed: a curved line glyph, a letter, a pattern, repeated precisely, endlessly the same but not the same.

the line
the letter
collection of letters, of lines
a word
a pattern
focused on a plane
between
what it is
and what it is not
what it looks like
at one moment
in time

(4V75 NYC)

What is the role of the line *in your work of art in this exhibition?*

Being a sculptor, line is immediately associated with the notion of verticality in the round and non-representationality. Consequently, it relates, immediately, to statuary, a word which comes from Latin *'stare'*, which means "standing up." It became, for me, more and more urgent to be able to express strong line in space, around which the viewer can turn. It was a way to survive.

What is the relationship between the work in this exhibition and your subsequent work?

Already, in the *Untitled* piece of 1973, the surface is hammered all over, which was a way for me to introduce a personal vibration and touch which removed me from the fabricated quality that Minimalism generally carries. That has been intensified with the indentation that we generally find toward the top of my recent vertical lines, which are sculptures. The range of my work developed from lines on the floor, lines on the wall, to the recent, 3-dimensional lines in the round.

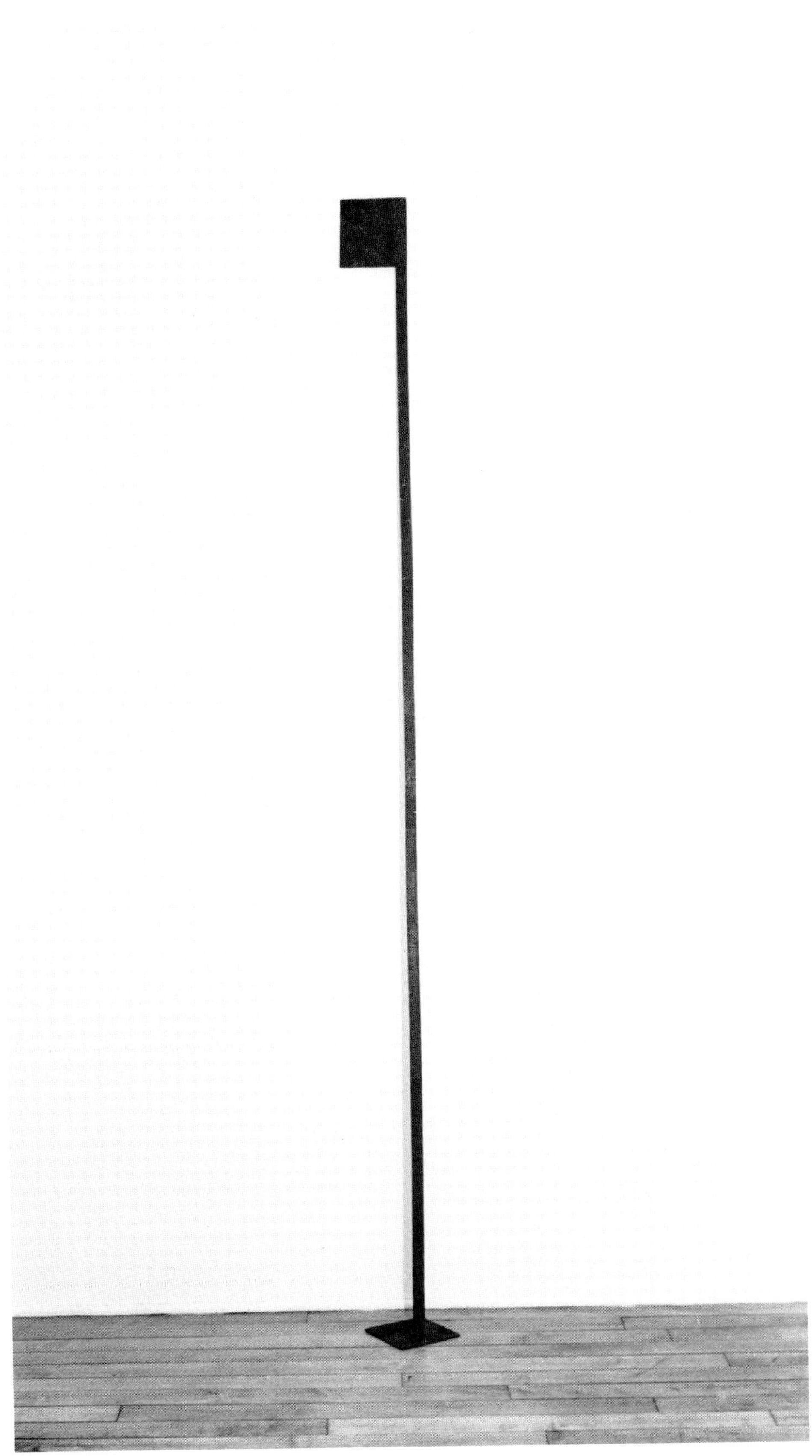

***Untitled*, 1973. Iron, 8′ × 1″. Lent courtesy the artist.**

William Wegman

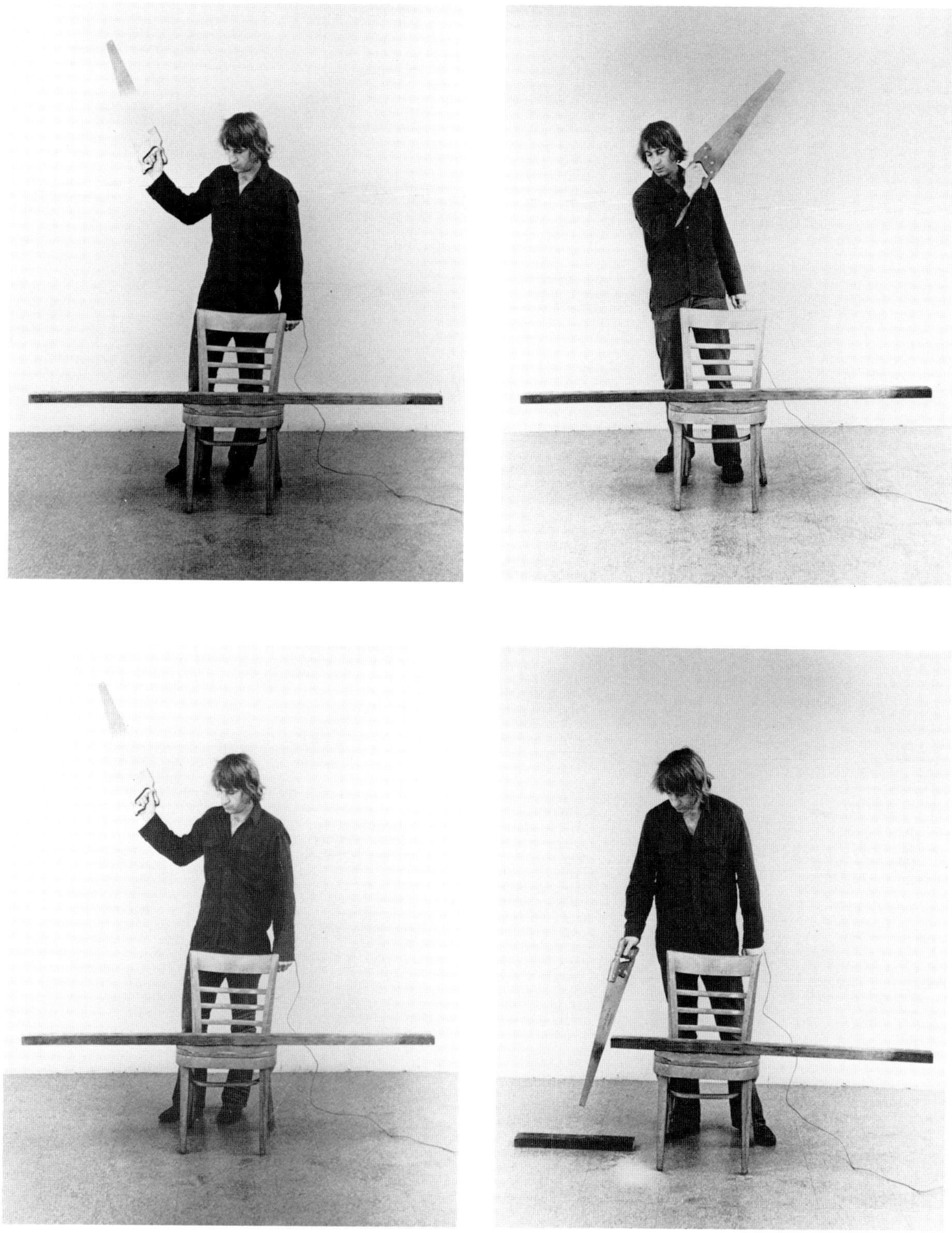

Four Panel Board Cutting Piece ("Electric Saw"), 1973. 4 photographs each 14 × 11". Lent courtesy Holly Solomon and the artist.

What is the role of the line *in your work of art in this exhibition?*

Interrupted sequences.

What is the relationship between the work in this exhibition and your subsequent work?

Typical.

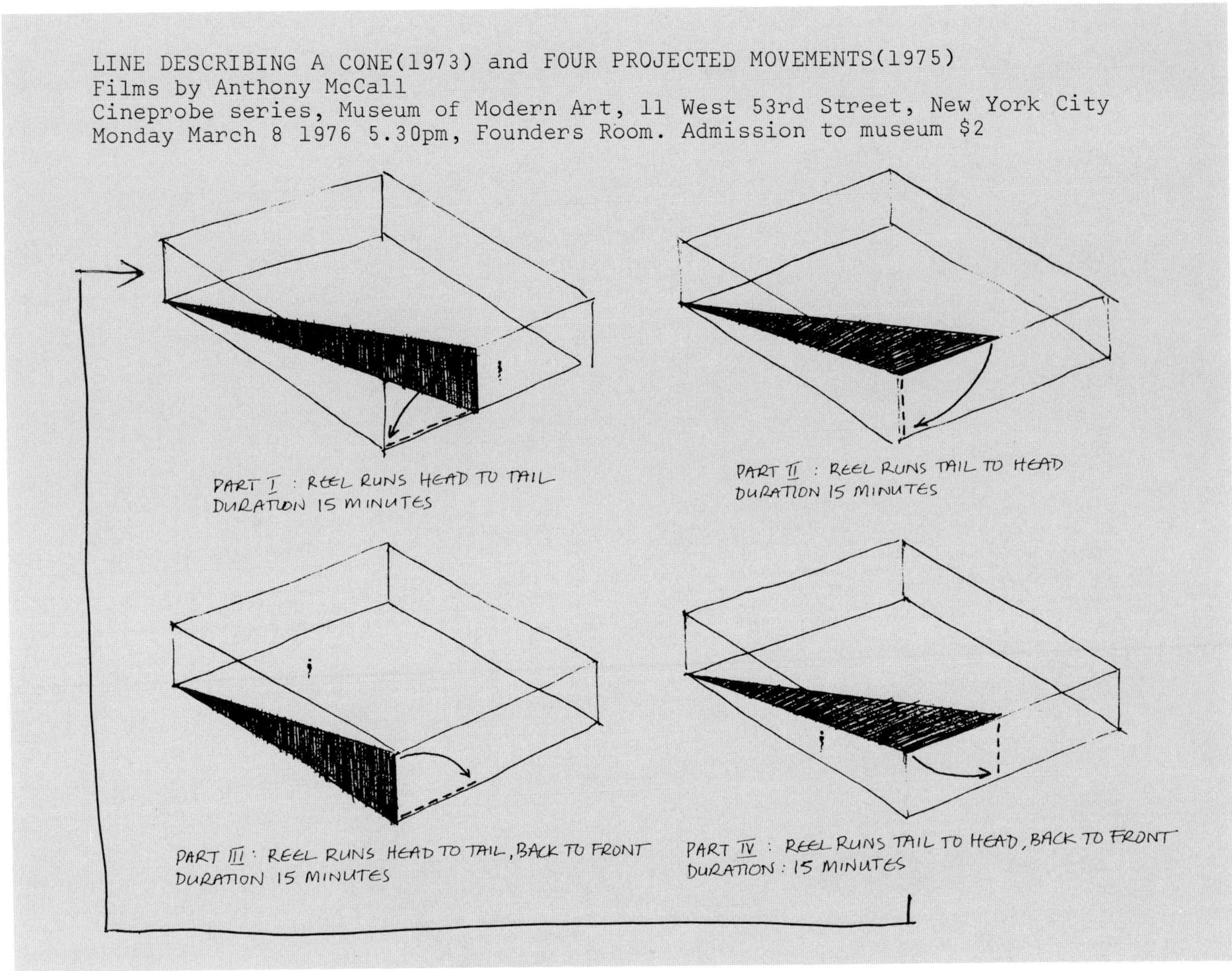

***Four Projected Movements,* 1975. Four working drawings on announcement cards**

Four Projected Movements 1975, New York. 16mm film

The four movements, each a 15-minute sweep of a plane of light through 90 degrees, result from a single 15-minute reel of film, passed through the projector in the four possible ways. The projector is positioned in a corner of a large empty room so that a wall and the floor establish the boundaries of the space through which the beams will travel. The cycle repeats through the duration of the presentation.

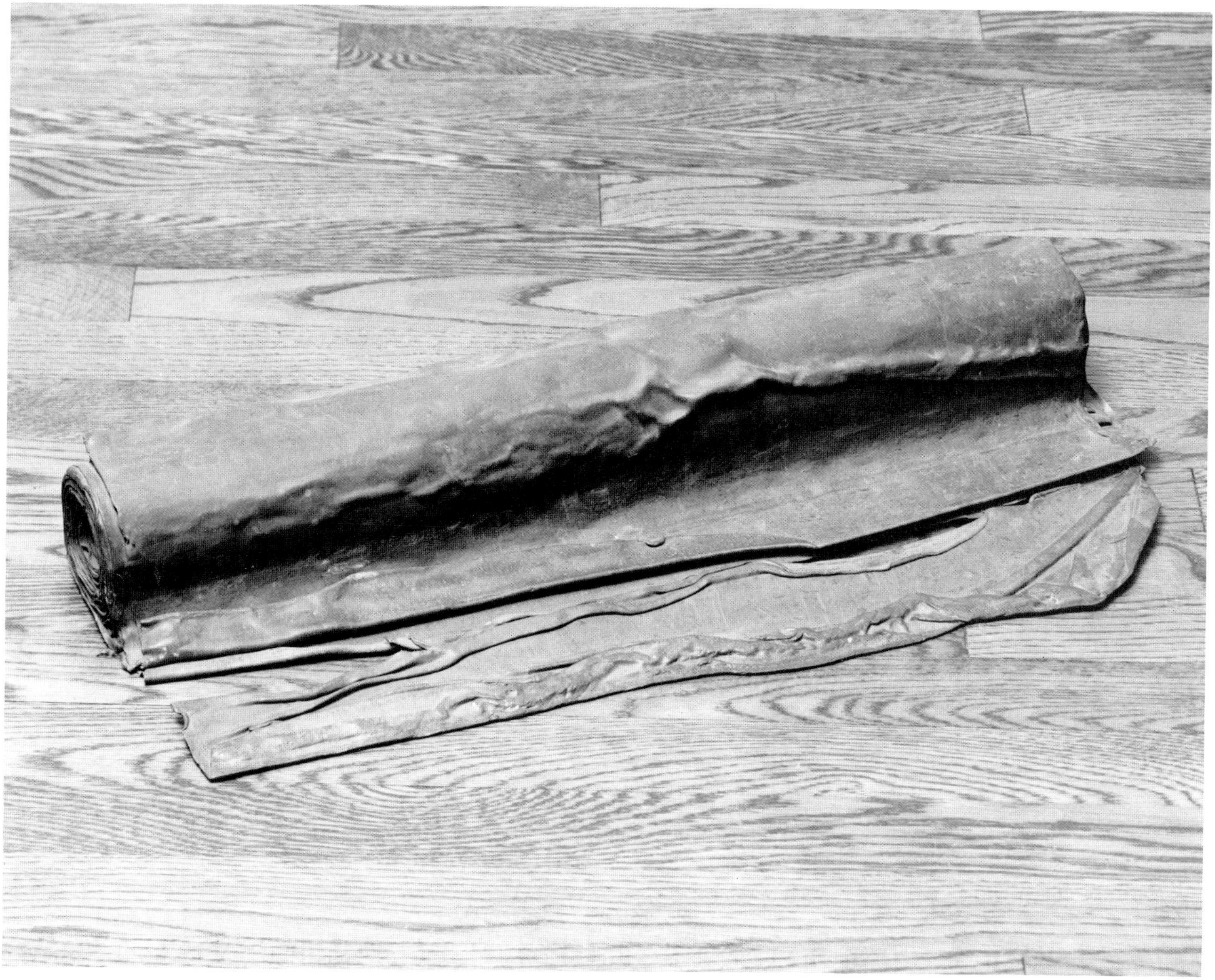

30 Feet of Rolled Lead, n.d. Lead; 3 × 24 × 10″. Lent courtesy Holly and Horace Solomon, NYC.

Shoot, 1971. Photo Mural; 48 × 96". Lent courtesy the artist and Ronald Feldman, Fine Arts, New York.

"*Shoot* was a performance which consisted in having a friend shoot me with a gun in the upper left arm. The trajectory of the bullet is in a straight line. This line was created in a very small fraction of a second."

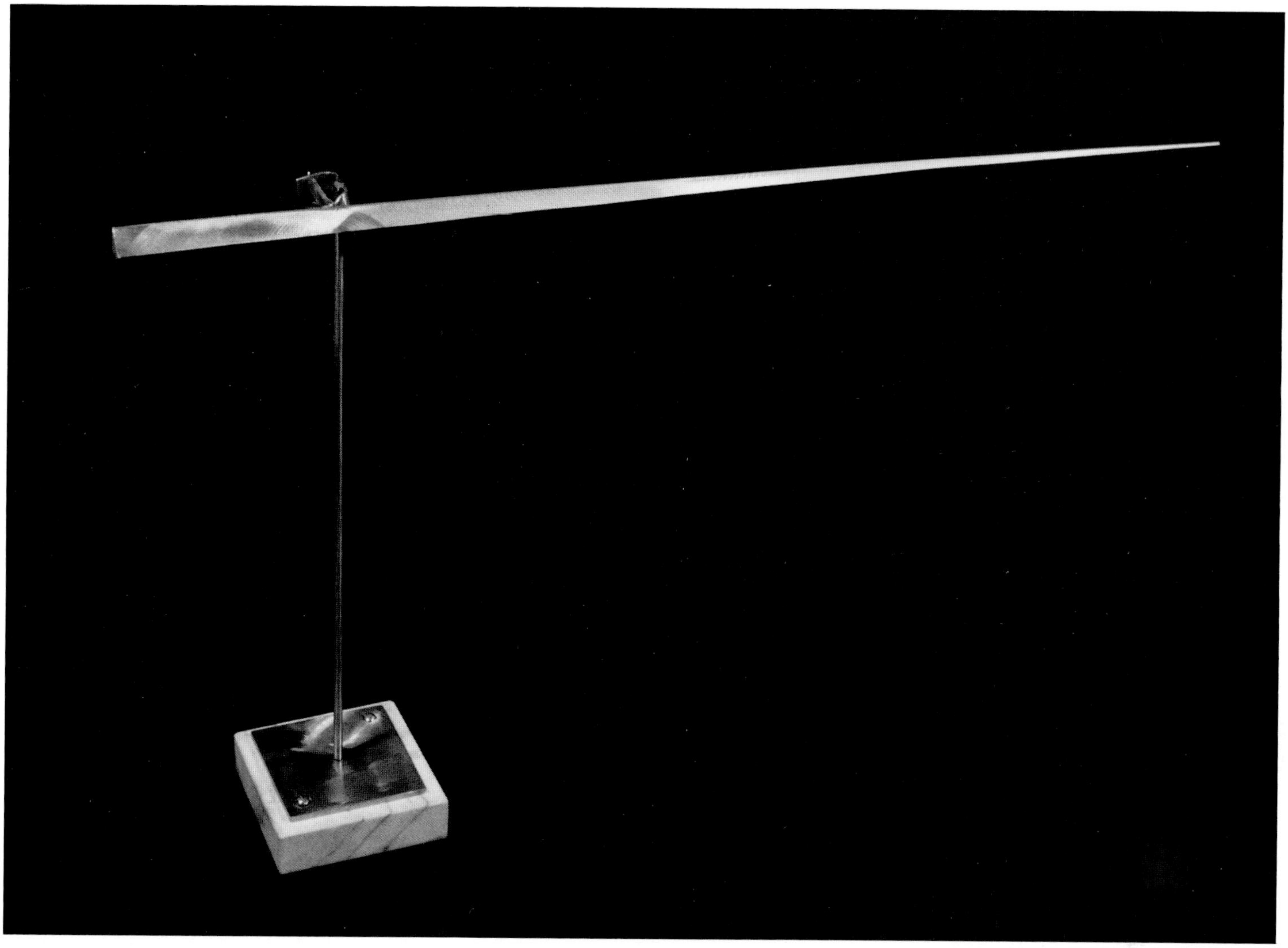

Single Line, 1964–70. Stainless steel, marble base; 11½ × 19 × 2½″. Lent courtesy Stuart Rickey.

Nulla dies Sine Linea

When I first began—about 1950—making constructions which moved, I began to find that figurative motifs were not for me, though they had been in most of my two previous decades as a painter. If movement was to be the expressive component, the *structure* which moved must be as unexpressive as possible. The example of Calder's wires, with their Miroesque sheet metal shapes attached, was before me. In an early piece I made similar linkages, with neat squares on the ends of the wires. Then I made some with nothing on the ends—just the wires, just lines.

In 1961 I abandoned the wires and made straight lines of folded slivers of stainless-steel sheet, creased along the middle for stiffness, tapered to a slender point. This became my pen-stroke, so to speak, with which diverse kinetic drawings could be made in space. Like a pen-stroke, it was heavy at one end, light at the other. I found a way to mount my steel stylus-stroke on knife-edge bearings, counterweighted at the wide end with lead cast into the V. Each line became a compound pendulum, whose natural period of swing I could control by distribution of the weight. Thus pen-stroke became time-stroke, usually with as slow a beat as I could manage. The force to set the lines in motion was a little breeze, even the draft of someone walking by. One line made a statement, two a dialogue, more a conversation, but never unison.

This began thirty years ago. The possibilities I have not yet exhausted. The pen-strokes I still employ, sometimes in clusters, sometimes doubled in open forms, sometimes widened as rectangles or triangles, sometimes vertical, sometimes horizontal, sometimes both with movement through a conical, instead of a planar, path. I even bent a single line into a circle and pivoted it between two points and mounted those two points on a pendulum in order to turn oscillation into rotation.

This sort of thing still goes on.

Lever, original 1966, reconstruction 1969. 137 firebricks; 4 × 9 × 3". Lent courtesy National Gallery of Canada, Ottawa/Galerie Nationale du Canada, Ottawa.

The art association is when the image is associated with things other than what the art work itself is. Art of isolation has its own micus with a minimum association with things not itself. The idea is the exact opposite of multi-media communication. My work is the exact opposite of the art of association. I try to reduce the image-making function of my work to the least degree.

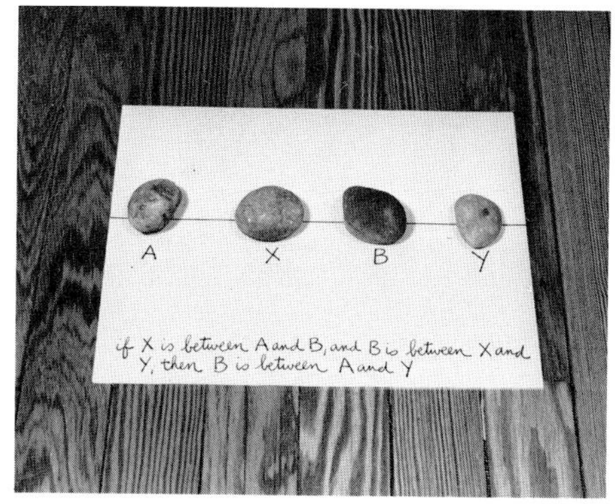

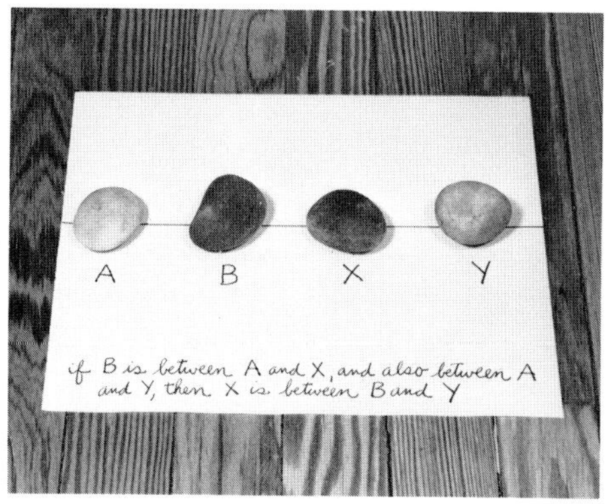

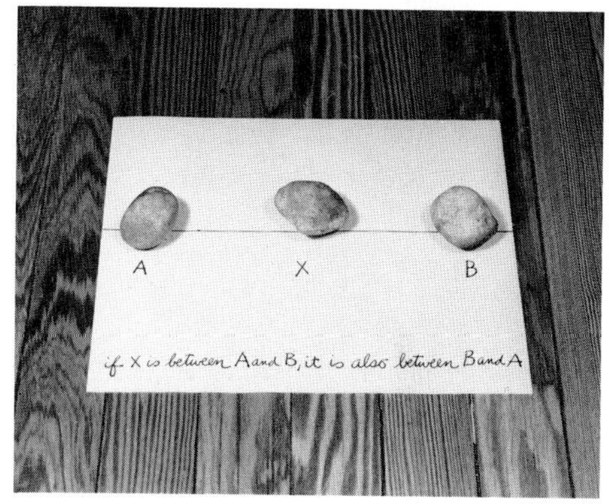

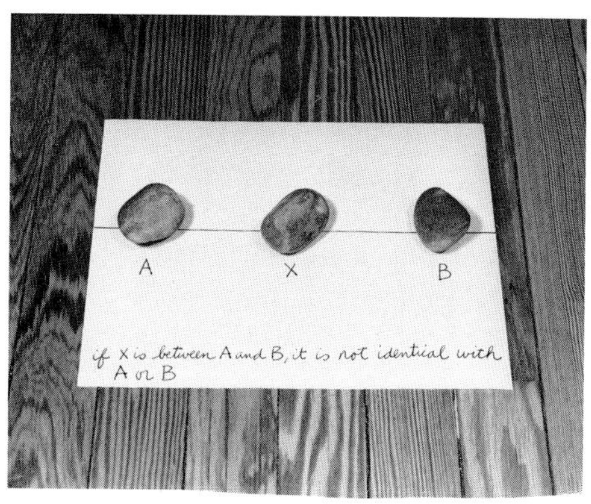

Seven Properties of Between, 1971–72.
Stones on paper on floor; 8½ × 110″.
Lent courtesy Sonnabend Gallery, NYC.

Forrest Myers

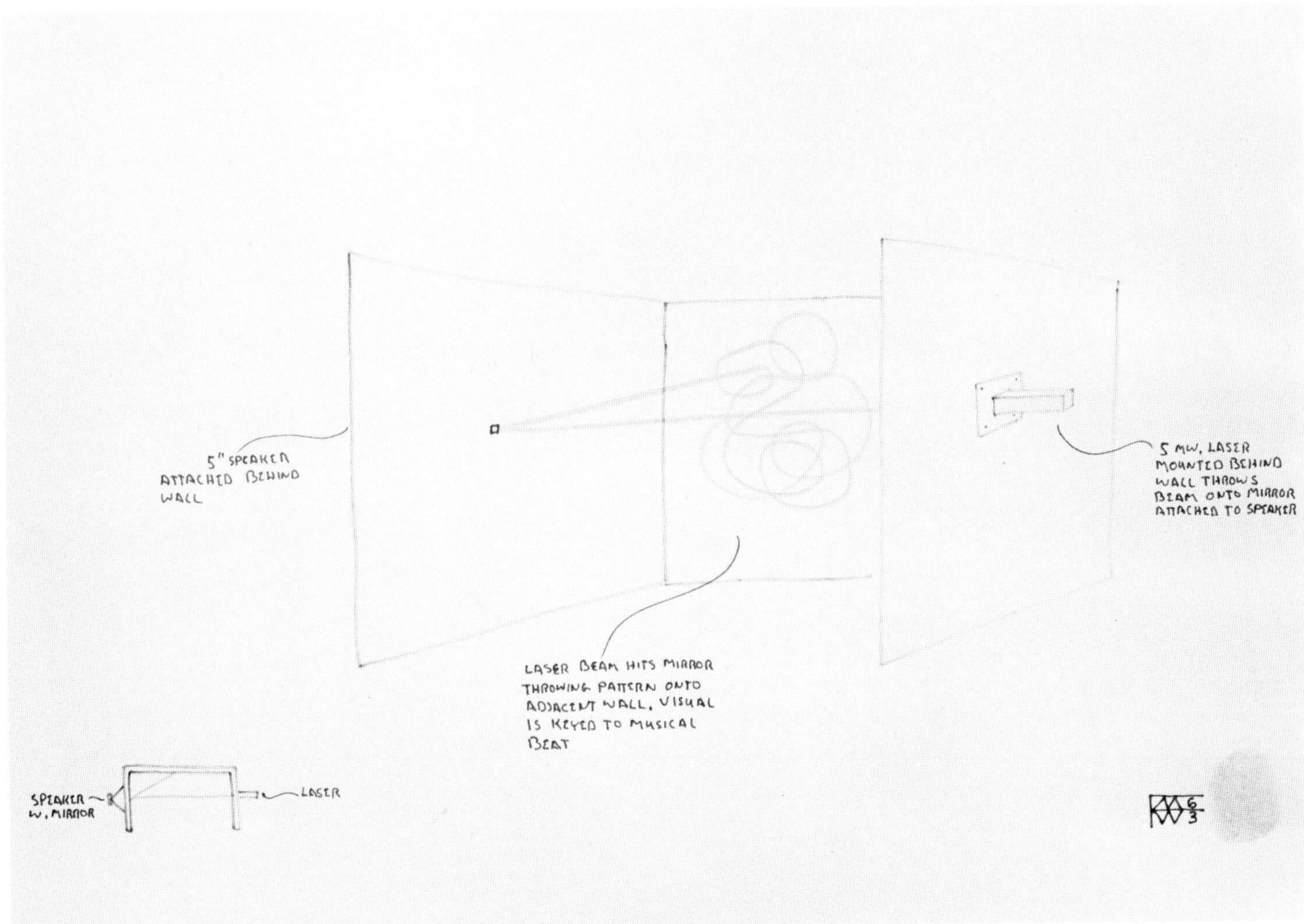

Laser with Speaker and Mirror, **1963. Ink on paper; 12 × 18". Lent courtesy the artist.**

What is the role of the line *in your work of art in this exhibition?*

These early laser pieces were simple attempts to explore some of the more obvious possibilities of the laser as a drawing tool. Whether it was using sound to generate a moving line or drawing lines that went through walls, the laser's columnated light seemed a premier tool for an artist working in a linear form.

What is the relationship between the work in this exhibition and your subsequent work?

My early line pieces included the stretching of stainless steel wires between buildings, using several carbon arc searchlights to construct static forms in the sky, and the use of lasers to draw lines. Yet I find myself concerned with the two basic things El Greco said interested him most in paintings, "light and line," another case of "The more things change the more they stay the same," I guess.

100 Boots Facing the Sea (a digression). Del Mar, California, February 9, 1971, 2:00 pm. Photograph; 9 × 12". Part of a series, *Walking the Line from "100 Boots."* Lent courtesy the artist and Ronald Feldman, Fine Arts, New York.

I thought of this work as a kind of long epistolary novel—it lasted over 2 1/2 years—presenting the adventures of a picaresque hero, *100 Boots.* The intervals between mailings of the individual images in the form of postcards varied with what I took to be the internal necessities of a narrative in process. It was this partially intuited narrative line to which each image or sequence of 5 to 10 cards aspired, that gave a forward thrust to the work—a kind of living line. Since installments of the narrative were interrupted by 1 to 4 week intervals between mailings, I like to think of this line as something of a dotted one.

But as this exhibition was concerned primarily with the literal sense of linearity, I was asked to include only those images which were arranged in a strictly linear fashion. I agreed because in many instances I had arranged the Boots in the landscape in the form of a simple geometric gestalts—arcs, triangles, straight lines—to insist upon their unity as a single heroic self with many feet. This tended, even in their geometric formations, to anthropomorphize and personalize them. It gave them a strong presence in the landscape. They weren't wimps.

Untitled #80.103, 1974. Black wool; 10′ × ½″. Lent courtesy DIA Foundation, NYC.

What is the role of the line *in your work of art in this exhibition?*

My choice of the line, as a physical entity— a piece of wool—was partly because of its pedestrian and malleable nature, the sculptural equivalent of a #2 pencil. It also seemed appropriate because of its approximate lack of an interior. It was possible to set up a more or less complicated situation without the inward-turning or closure inherent in planar or volumetric materials.

What is the relationship between the work in this exhibition and your subsequent work?

My more recent work has tended to be less bound to particular architectural elements or details (as opposed to the overall given architectural situation).

Dennis Oppenheim

During the beginning of Land Art in the late sixties, sculptural domain extended to include horizontal expanse rather than the more traditional focus on volume and mass. Works of art, on land, tended to "activate" large spaces. My use of line within this context was usually related more to "drawing," or more specifically, *inscribing*.

Quite often, my works were located between boundaries of countries, thereby including, or tapping into the real world, with so-called abstract gesture (see *Time Line*).

The works shown in this exhibition are somewhat ephemeral, and function more as indications of "process" and physical force. This follows a long interest in the methods involved in acts of art making; its origins, its problems in objectification, and more specifically the deterioration of concept, as the work progressively becomes more concrete. I like my early sculptures to exist *between* a state of ignition and solidifaction.

Time Line, 1968. Boundary between U.S.A./Canada, St. John River; Fort Kent Maine. 1 × 3 × 3′ cut between two countries. Lent courtesy the artist.

Robert Barry

Moving Line, 0° – 350° × 50°, 1968.
Ink on paper; 8 pieces each 11 × 8.5″.
Lent courtesy the artist.

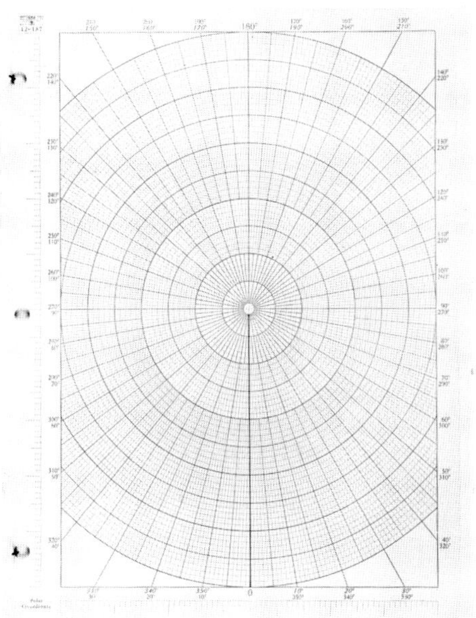

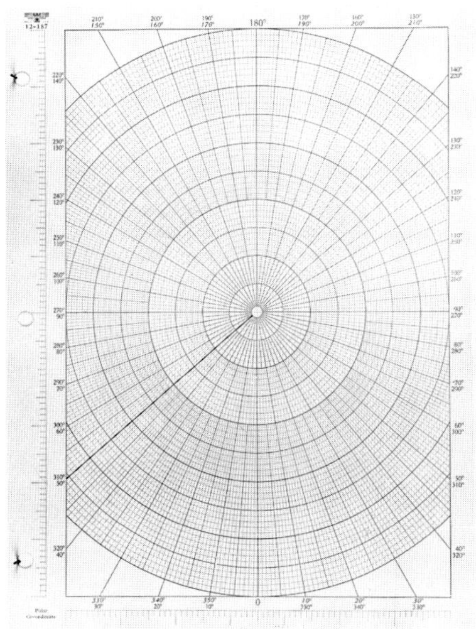

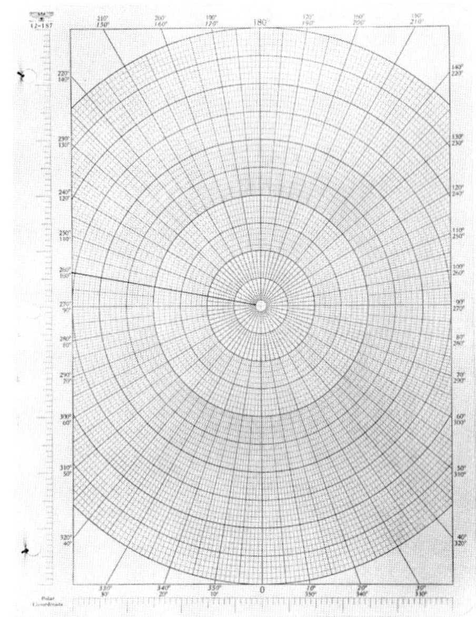

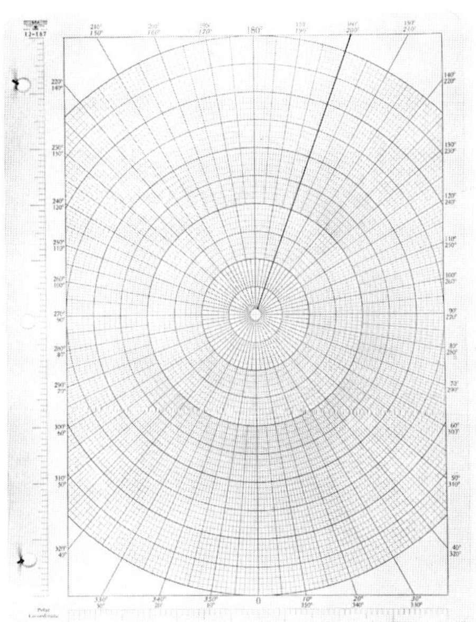

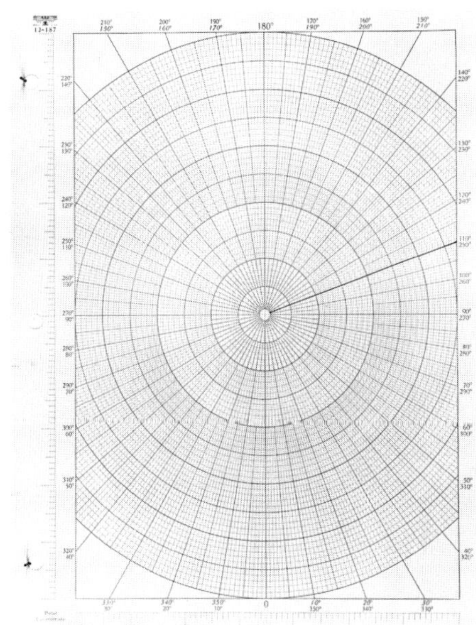

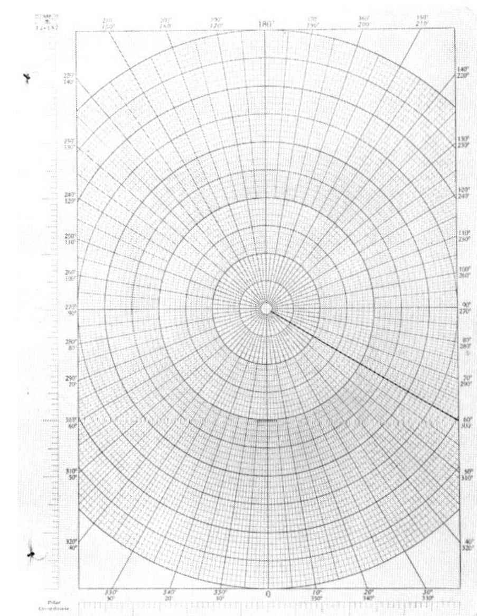

What is the role of the line *in your work of art in this exhibition?*

I used the 'line' as an indication of time passing, movement, direction, description, and the space between things.

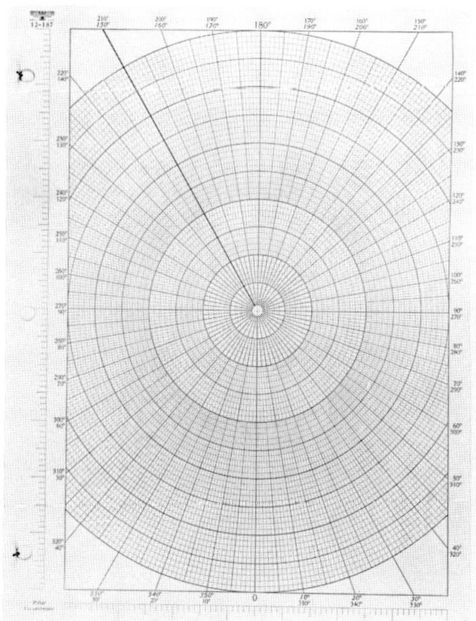

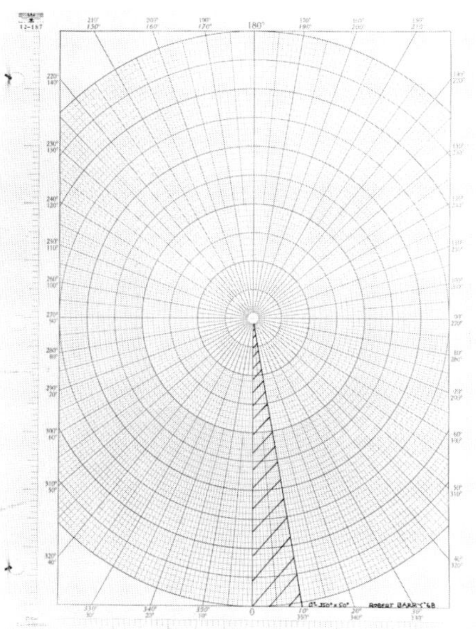

It is . . . It isn't . . ., 1972. Ink on paper; Lent courtesy the artist.

It is... it isn't...

It is allowed,
questionable,
vulnerable,
changeable,
persistent,
subjective,
limited,
tenuous,
individual,
conditioned,
insufficient,
contradictory,
active,
adjusted,
restricted,
involved,
precarious,
allusive,
fragile,
arranged,
influenced,
doubted,
public,
dependent,
presented,
flexible,
affected,
dubious,
tentative,
varied,
divisible,
diverse,
elusive,
derivative,
continuing,
improbable and
it isn't unaffected,
isolated,
empty,
arbitrary,
enough,
permanent,
precise,
proven,
accidental,
necessary,
concealed,
purposeful,
rigid,
decided,
explicit,
reliable,
clarified,
insistent,
essential,
defined,
direct,
constant,
assured,
emphatic,
secure,
inevitable,
certain,
closed,
explained,
adequate,
absolute,
established,
exact,
definite,
conclusive
or finished...

Crazy Otto, 1962. Oil on canvas; 66 × 65″. Lent courtesy The Pace Gallery, NYC.

What is the role of the line *in your work of art in this exhibition?*

Instead of being used to outline something, this line divides the Rocky Mountain watershed into two parts, West and East. While the landscape of snow, and mountains remains essentially passive, the line, composed of lichen-covered rocks, becomes an active sculptural presence.

What is the relationship between the work in this exhibition and your subsequent work?

The writing in these "art documentations" gradually became more narrative in my work and began to tell a story rather than describe the photographs. I did other kinds of lines, as in my thrown rope series where flowers were planted where a thrown rope landed ("4-part Thrown Rope Piece," American Pavilion, Venice Biennale, 1980). Now, in my "Mountain Grammar" series, the only lines are written ones.

***Continental Divide,* 1970. Print—photographs and silkscreen; 30 × 20". Lent courtesy the artist.**

Cut Line, 1971. Kraft Paper, tape, corrugated board, ink; closed: 7½ × 7½ × 39", open: 36 × 720". Lent courtesy the artist.

What is the role of the line *in your work of art in this exhibition?*

"Cut Line" as an instrument of measure: For the "Gedok" exhibition "Cut Line" was severed in several places to accommodate walls and other obstacles. It lay flat on the floor. Not only measuring, but activating and "ruling" the surface. Its entire length determining not the length of the floors, but establishing an awareness of a measure. Hence, duration of the sculpture represents both a "possession" and a "measure" of the surface.

What is the relationship between the work in this exhibition and your subsequent work?

Reviewing more than ten years of my work "the line" in my drawings functions as a mapping or charting device or as an indicator of the possibility of movement or shift—interlock—expansion and contraction. Pouring, cutting, excavating, marking (in a variety of ways), are some of the means by which "the line" as an abstraction has been given a physicality in my sculpture.

Whereas, "the line" has provided and enabled: measure, movement, direction, alignment, separation and joining, line-up, expansion, contraction, shift, marking, demarcation, correspondence, and also a means for locking information into place—foremost for me, the Maximal Implications of "the line" has been as a metaphor, a sounding line—a plumb line.

Locator with Mirror, 1972. Steel 2″ I pipe; 5 × 1′. Lent courtesy John Weber Gallery, NYC.

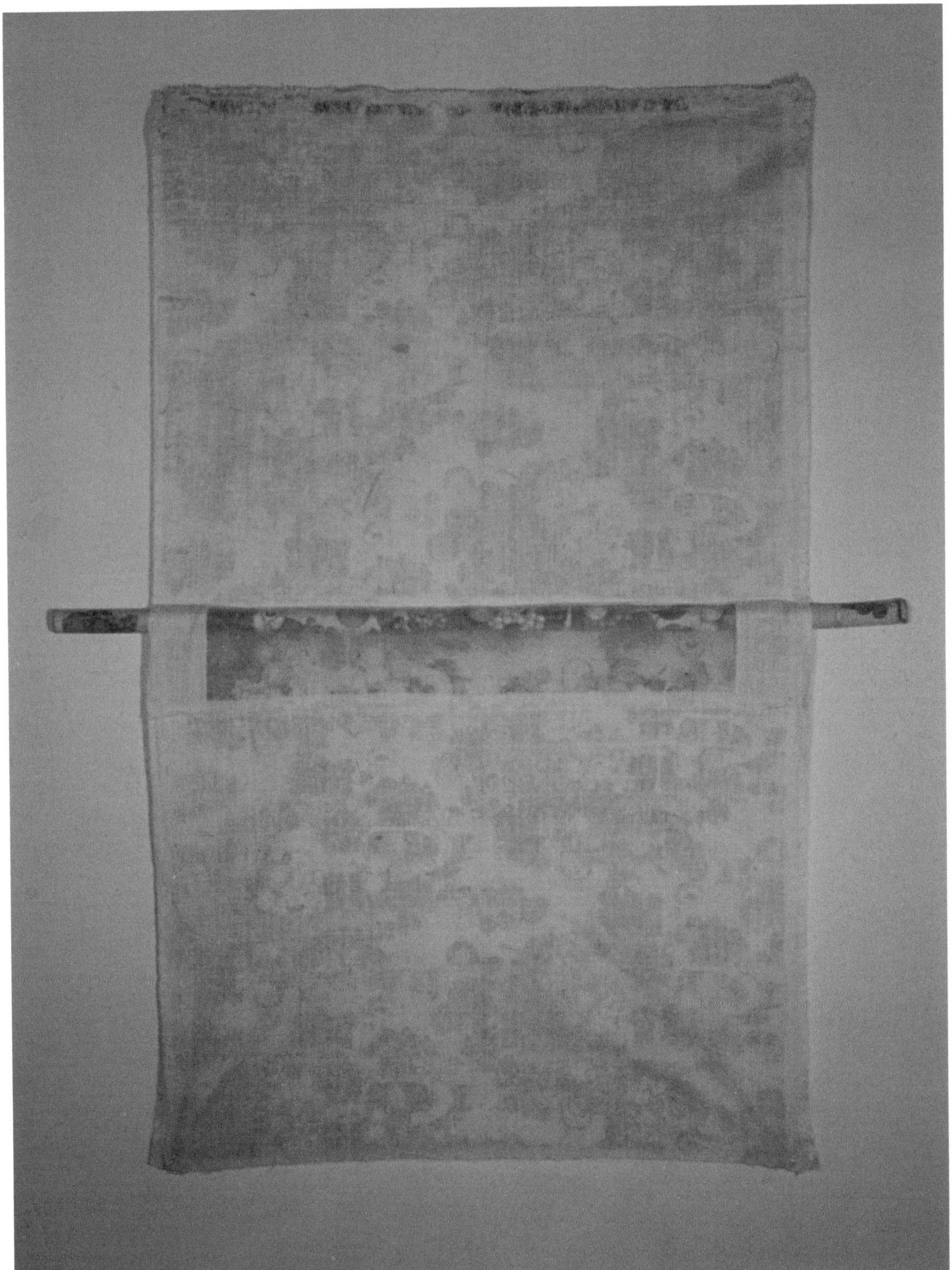

Jackpot (Jammer #386), 1975. Fabric and wood, 74½ × 60¼″. Lent courtesy Leo Castelli Gallery.

Running Fence, Sonoma and Marin Counties, California, **1972–76. Color photographs; 26¼ × 39¼". Lent courtesy the artist.**

Running Fence, 18 ft. high, 24.1/2 miles long, extending East-West near Freeway 101, north of San Francisco, on the private properties of 59 ranchers, following the rolling hills and dropping down to the Pacific Ocean at Bodega Bay, was completed on September 10. 1976. The art project consisted of: 42 months of collaborative efforts, the ranchers' participation, 18 public hearings, 3 sessions at the Superior Courts of California, the drafting of a 450 page environmental impact report and the temporary use of the hills, the sky and the ocean. Conceived and financed by Christo, Running Fence was made of 165,000 yards of heavy woven white nylon fabric, hung from a steel cable strung between 2,050.steel poles (each: 21 ft.long,3".1/2 diameter) embedded 3 ft. into the ground, using no concrete and braced laterally with guy wires (90 miles of steel cable) and 14,000. earth anchors. The top and bottom edges of the 2,050 fabric panels were secured to the upper and lower cables by 350,000. hooks. All parts of Running Fence's structure were designed for complete removal and no visible evidence of Running Fence remains on the hills of Sonoma and Marin Counties.

As it had been agreed with the ranchers and with county, state and federal agencies, the removal of Running Fence started 14 days after its completion and all materials were given to the ranchers. Running Fence crossed 14 roads and the town of Valley Ford, leaving passage for cars, cattle and wildlife, and was designed to be viewed by following 40 miles of public roads, in Sonoma and Marin Counties.

Chop, 1971. Wood; 16 × 12″ × 30′. Lent courtesy the artist.

What is the role of the line in your work of art in this exhibition?

Those lines shape space, cut it, activate. That broken line changes the place it's in: lowers it, thickens it, slows it down. It is an object that becomes a place.

What is the relationship between the work in this exhibition and your subsequent work?

Those early pieces showed me what accented space could do, how simple objects could change the world I moved in. Everything since, comes out of that.

What is the role of the line *in your work of art in this exhibition?*

The highly polished stainless-steel works I made in the latter 1960s achieved a kind of dualism through the mirror-like finish of their surfaces. The inherent properties of steel—weightiness, physicality—are confounded by the reflective aspects of the surface which allows the form, under certain lighting conditions, to virtually disappear into its environment. What remains visible is a network of lines which indicate the interior faces of the sculpture.

What is the relationship between the work in this exhibition and your subsequent work?

In my subsequent work, I have tried to maintain a balance between the obvious monumental and physical aspects of my forms and their own sense of internal logic. I try to make works which have a powerful presence but are also self-reflective and able to establish a rich communication with their environment.

***Torre Pieno Nel Vuoto,* 1969. Stainless steel; 95 × 20 × 40″. Lent courtesy the artist.**

What is the role of the line *in your work of art in this exhibition?*

The work itself is a line, but it is not only a line: it is an incomplete square. The site is very important: the edge of the wall has to be parallel to the vertical pink neon line. This helps the viewer complete the square in his or her imagination.

What is the relationship between the work in this exhibition and your subsequent work?

This is a characteristic work of mine for the period, and the period was a very important one for me. My subsequent work has continued the development of incomplete squares and incomplete circles. First the same shape might be fragmented, as two arcs making up part of the same incomplete circle. Then, incomplete squares and circles might be combined in the same work. More recently, wavy lines and distorted incomplete circles and squares have been introduced. But there is still the strong connection to earlier works such as this one.

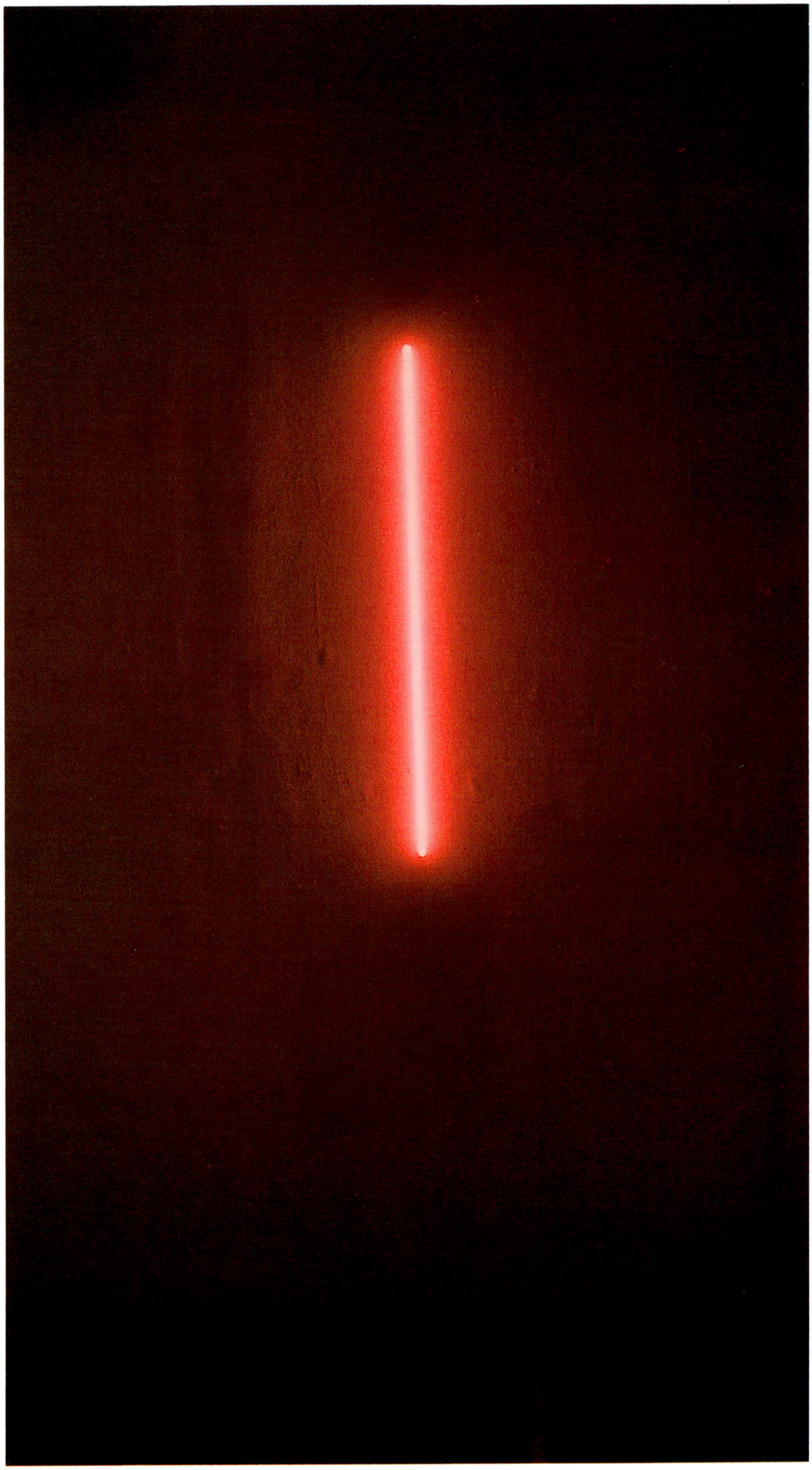

***Incomplete Pink Neon Square,* 1974. Neon tube + transformer; 3′ × 3″. Lent courtesy Jane Logemann and Gerry Rosen.**

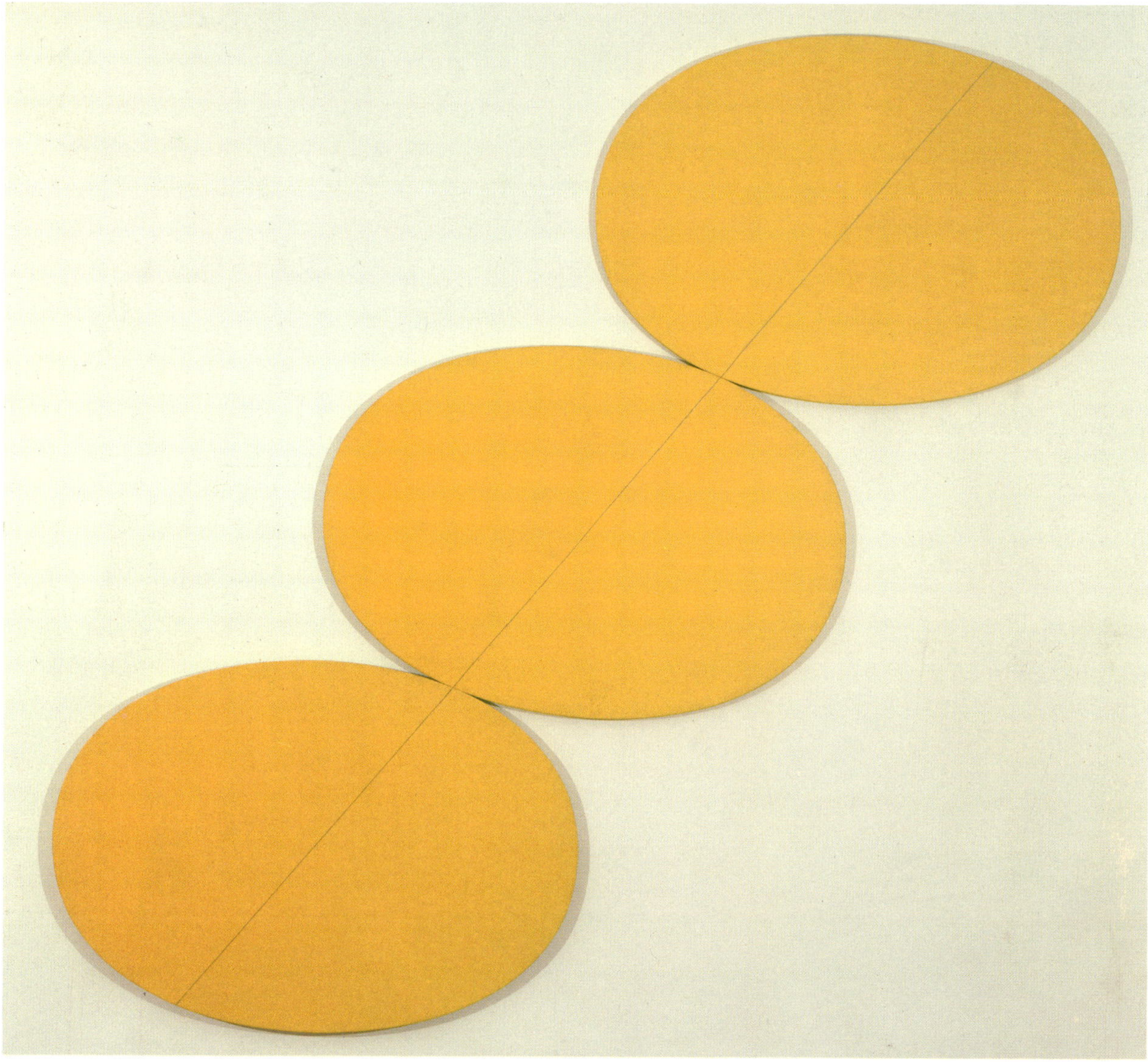

Constellation: Three Yellow Ovals, **1967. Acrylic on canvas, 105 × 52". Lent courtesy Washburn Gallery, NYC.**

What is the role of the line *in your work of art in this exhibition?*

The role of the line in this painting is multiple in its responsibilities: it is home base for the wanderer of the spaces about it, it regulates the speed of movement, it is a reverberator for the forces of energy which build up about it and it demands directional decision at each intersection. The line is "in and out," "back and forth," "above and below," as well as "up and down," and it is the crack in the door when opening and closing.

What is the relationship between the work in this exhibition and your subsequent work?

This painting, *Three Yellow Ovals,* from the "Constellation" series is merely a step between the "Correspondence" series and the subsequent work in the evolutionary development of my search and research of space and force.

First Working Drawing for Gradient Field II. 1977. Strathmore 3-ply bond paper, vellum, sanguine and conte: 30 × 40″. Lent courtesy Xavier Fourcade, Inc.

Douglas Huebler

The line above is rotating on its axis at a speed of one revolution each day

The Line Represented Above These Words is Rotating at the Rate of One Revolution Per Day, **1968–69. Typeface. Lent courtesy the artist.**

What is the role of the line *in your work of art in this exhibition?*

There are actually *two* lines in this piece: One may be *seen* as its presence manifests itself as visual fact, while the other "line"—the percipient's "center of gravity"—is equally present, although it cannot be seen. During that Sisyphean instant when the percipient senses the simultaneous presence of both lines he/she is engaged in an act of "self-production" which is, in itself, the virtual subject of this work.

What is the relationship between the work in this exhibition and your subsequent work?

In all more recent work the structure is similar although the visual elements now range from photographs to other representational modes (drawing, painting, sculpture, etc.) while the language has become more narrative, including both "anecdote," and "aphorism," as dialectical components. (Rather than try to elaborate further I will resort to an old cliche: "a picture is worth a thousand words.")

What is the role of the line *in your work of art in this exhibition?*

The line operates in two ways: diagrammatic—presenting the architect's concept (an obelisk)—and expressive—what it would be like to see the monument in its natural surroundings.

What is the relationship between the work in this exhibition and your subsequent work?

I think I have taken the sort of hybrid described under the first question and driven it to greater extremes.

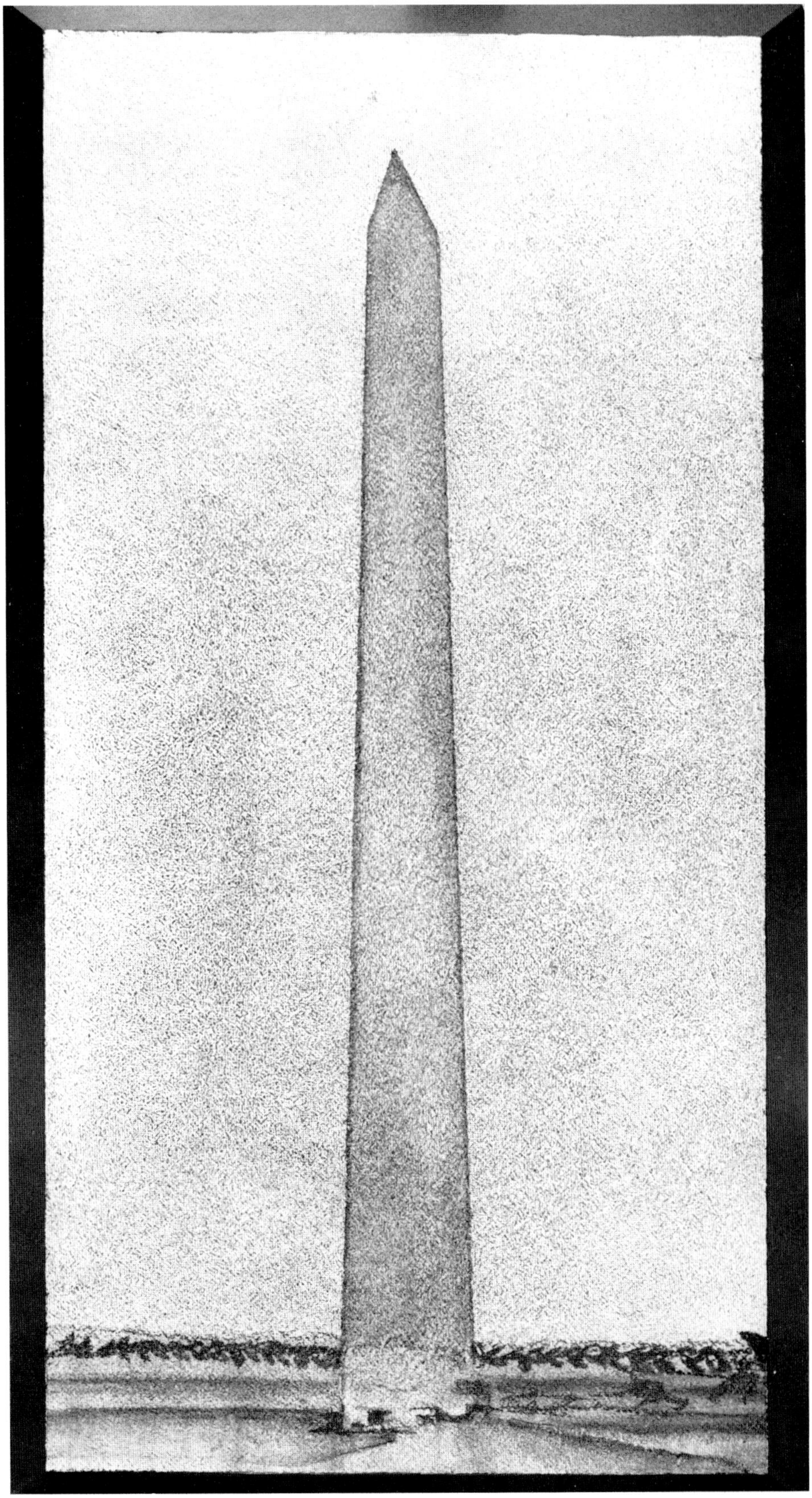

Washington Monument, 1964. Liquitex on celotex; 47 × 26″. Lent courtesy Norman Dolph.

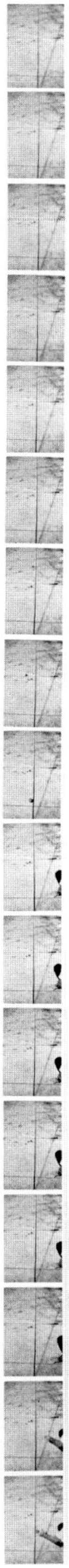

What is the role of the line *in your work of art in this exhibition?*

There are two lines involved in each work. The *ideal line* and the (hand-activated roll of the ball and disk) *attempted line*, positioned by the recording of the camera at four shots per second. The *length* of both lines is determined by the height of the film plane. The *number* of images in each attempt is determined by the speed of the roll, by the predetermined number of shots per second, and by the height of the film plane. But the most fascinating aspect is the role of perspective and how the camera records this phenomenon.

What is the relationship between the work in this exhibition and your subsequent work?

A major portion of my work has been and is concerned with attempting things that cannot ideally be realized. One aspect of this concern is aligning improbable things (not normally aligned) with an ideal line.

***Trying to Roll a Ball in a Straight Line from Bottom to Top and Top to Bottom (4 Photographs Per Second),* 1973.**
Color photographs; 110 × 5″. Lent courtesy Sonnabend Gallery, NYC and the artist.

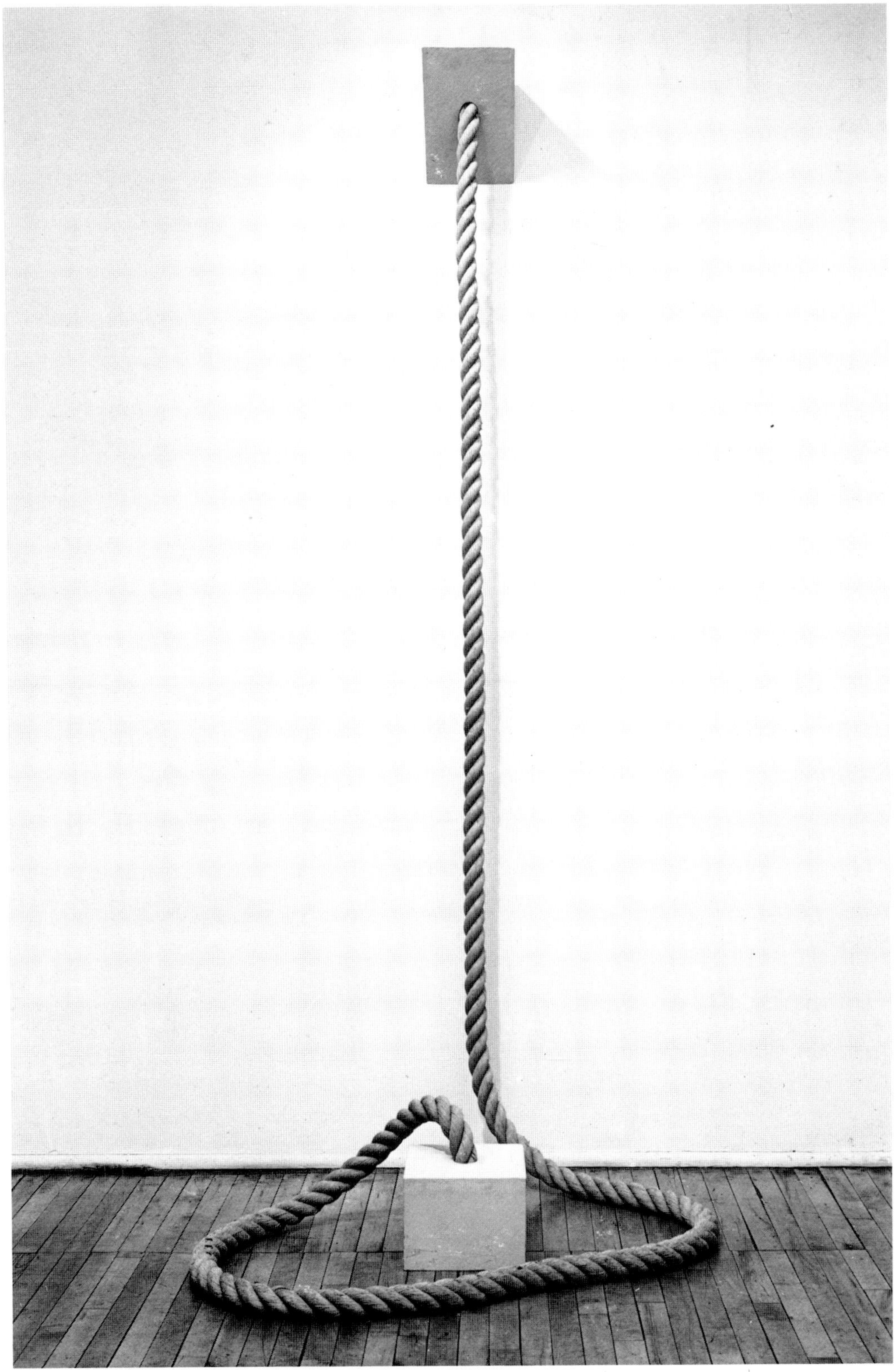

Rope Piece, 1964 (reconstructed 1984).
Rope and wood blocks; 219 × 10 × 10″.
Lent courtesy the artist.

Henry Flynt

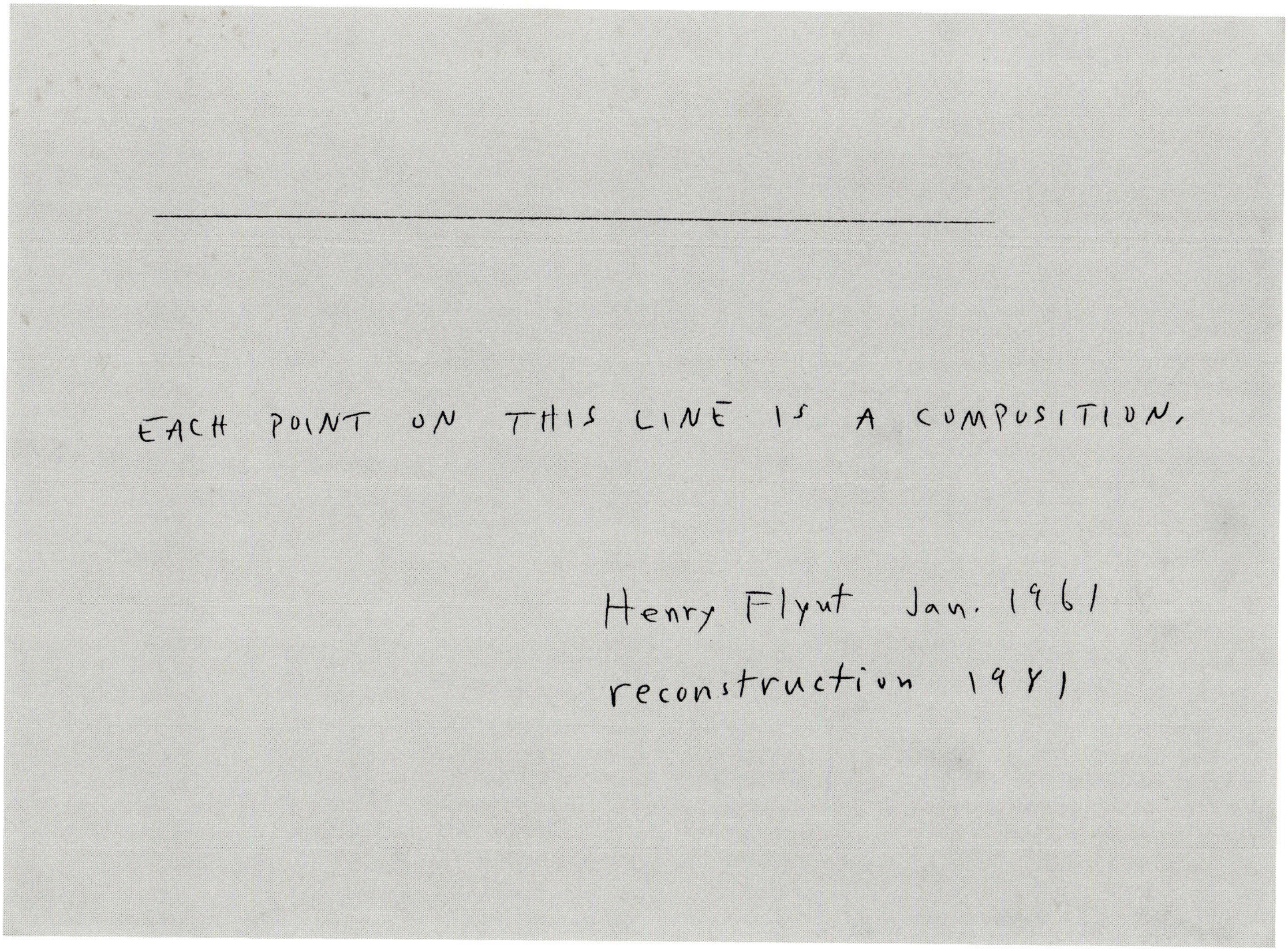

What is the role of the line *in your work of art in this exhibition?*

Since Cantor, the rectilinear continuum is considered to be a set of uncountably many points. "Each point on this line is a composition" is conceptual. By stipulating each point on the rectilinear segment as a composition, I authored uncountably many compositions. A further refinement is that it has not been resolved whether any real-world continuum, such as the drawing, is in fact limitlessly subdivisible as claimed for the abstract line.

What is the relationship between the work in this exhibition and your subsequent work?

This is one of a series of works I did after seeing L. Young's "word pieces" in Dec. 1960. It evinces the egoistic impulse to author an uncountable number of works; and also evinces by focus on imputing mathematical structures to visual apparitions which culminated in my "Concept Art" of mid-1961. I destroyed the original, along with many other works; the present work is a reconstruction made for a 1982 show.

An additional feature of the work is that it challenges the tenet of semiotics that linguistic expressions are countable.

Each Point on This Line is a Composition, **January 1961 (reconstruction 1981). Ink on paper; 28 × 21.6 cm. Lent courtesy The Gilbert and Lila Silverman Fluxus Collection.**

What is the role of the line *in your work of art in this exhibition?*

The line is the whole work in this case.

What is the relationship between the work in this exhibition and your subsequent work?

During the period in which these "string" paintings were made, there were also a number of two-sided grids being made. The end view of the grids is a simple line, so I made these string works to show a constant end view!

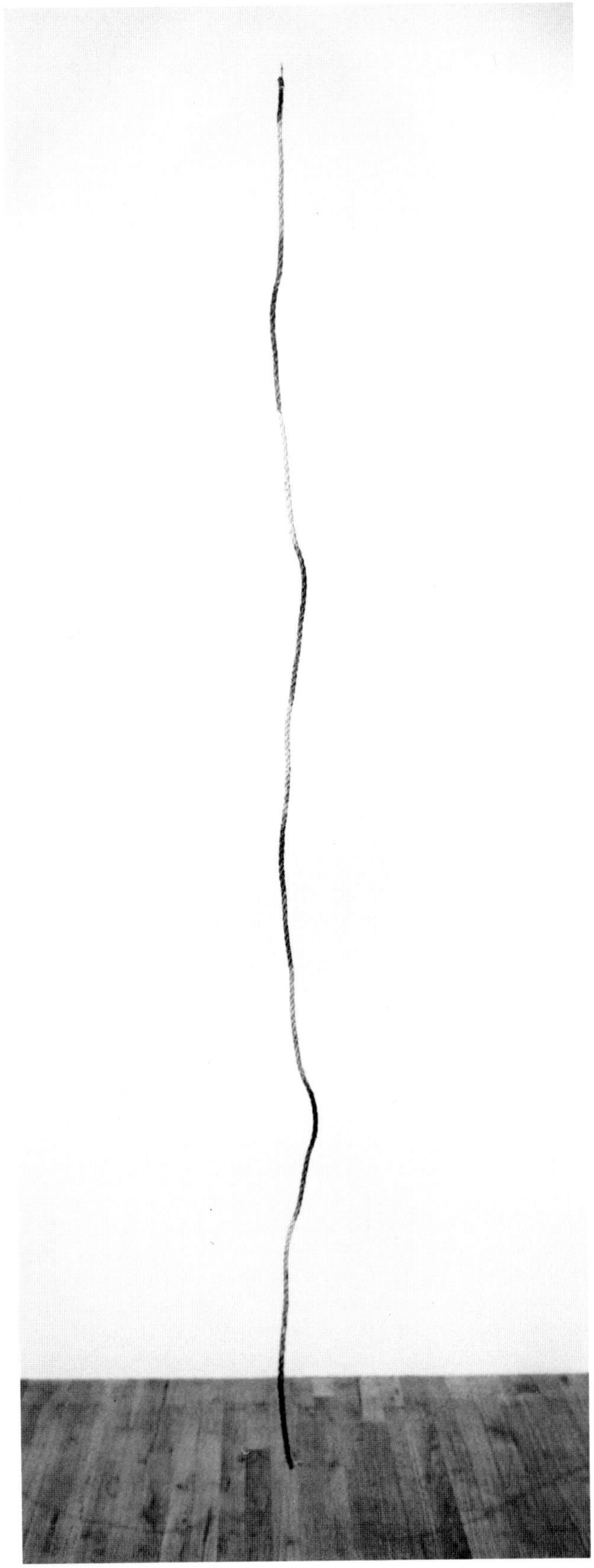

Rope Painting, 1969–70. Acrylic on rope; 114 × 3/8". Lent courtesy Paula Cooper Gallery, NYC.

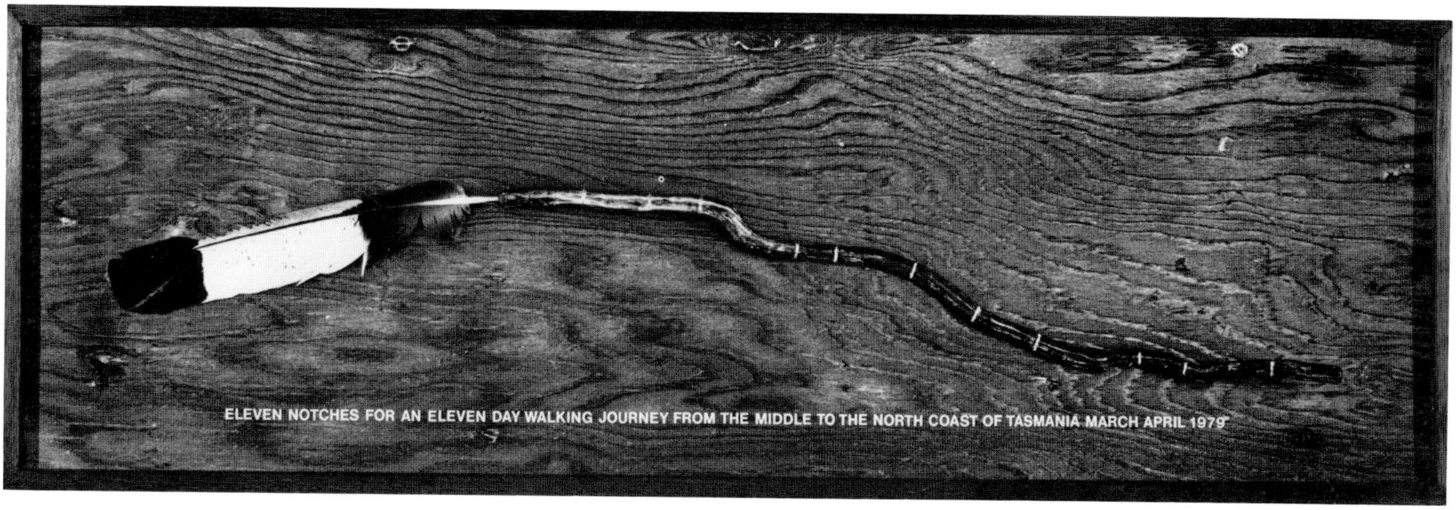

***Eleven Notches for an Eleven Day Walking Journey from the Middle to the North Coast of Tasmania*, 1979. Photograph; 10¾ × 31¾". Lent courtesy private collection.**

The Journey

My artform is the short journey—made by walking in the landscape.

It's An Indoor Life, It's An Indoor World

My artworks are made to be viewed in cities but ultimately they point to nature. The natural world was not made by humans. The greatest confrontation in the second half of the 20th century is between the urban mind and the natural mind.

Untitled, 1968. Blue lacquer on galvanized iron; 5 × 40 × 9″. Lent courtesy DIA Art Foundation, NYC.

Zen for TV (copy no. 4/12), 1963/75. Altered GE T.V. set; 21 × 16 × 13″. Lent courtesy The Gilbert and Lila Silverman Fluxus Collection.

(1)

My experimental TV is
not always interesting
but
not always uninteresting
like nature, which is beautiful,
not because it changes beautifully,
but simply because it changes.

(afterlude to the *Exposition of Experimental Television* 1963, March. Gallery Parnass.)

Second dimension of variability.

13 sets suffered 13 sorts of variation in their VIDEO-HORIZONTAL-VERTICAL units. I am proud to be able to say that all 13 sets actually changed their inner circuits. No two sets had the same kind of technical operation. Not one is the simple blur, which occurs when you turn the vertical and horizontal control-button at home. I enjoyed very much the study of electronics, which I began in 1961, and some life-danger I met while working with 15 Kilo-Volts. . . .

Many mystics are interested to spring out from ONE-ROW-TIME, ONE-WAY-TIME, in order to

GRASP the Eternity.

To stop at the consummated or sterile Zero-point is a classical method to grasp the eternity. . . .

My TV is more (?) than the art,
or
less (?) than the art.
I can compose something, which lies
higher (?) than my
personality,
or
lower (?) than my
personality.

What is the role of the line *in your work of art in this exhibition?*

Line can contain at once the rare paradox of stasis and motion, that is its role in my work of this period, coupled with its reductive simplicity as a foil for multiplicity of marks and its ability with scale to physically enjoin the viewer.

What is the relationship between the work in this exhibition and your subsequent work?

The relationship between the work in this exhibit and the works that follow is complex, but surely it is organic in a substantive way. It is always a path.

***Niagara Gorge Path Relocated,* 1975. Rocks, earth on muslin backed paper; 460′ × 5′2″. Lent courtesy the artist.**

Comet, December 24, 1973. Watercolor, ink on newspaper; 23 × 33″. Lent courtesy Barbara Gladstone Gallery, NYC.

I like to work in a way that people mis-see. I like people to mis-see. I like puns. I like them to mis-hear. I think Arthur Koestler said something about mistakes being the route to creativity. I notice that in myself. I make a mistake—I mis-see or I mis-hear—and it's much more creative than had I understood it correctly. If I can possibly provoke an instance for people where it can happen spontaneously, I want it to happen.

(printed with permission from the Barbara Gladstone Gallery.)

Checklist of the Exhibition

Cecile Abish. *Cut Line,* 1971. Kraft Paper, tape, corrugated board, ink; closed: 7½ × 7½ × 39", open: 36 × 720". Lent courtesy the artist.

Vito Acconci. *Following Piece,* 1969. Activity (street, people, pursuit). 23 days, varying durations New York City ("Street Works IV" Architectural League of New York). Lent courtesy the artist.

Vito Acconci. *Lay of the Land,* 1969. Laying down on my side, in an open field; a camera aimed out, toward the open field: I'm holding the camera first at my head, then at my chest, then at my stomach, then at my knees, then at my feet—a photograph is snapped from each position. Five black and white photographs; 20 × 20". Lent courtesy the artist and Michael Klein, Inc.

Carl Andre. *Lever,* original 1966, reconstruction 1969. 137 firebricks; 4 × 9 × 3". Lent courtesy National Gallery of Canada, Ottawa/Galerie Nationale du Canada, Ottawa.

Eleanor Antin. *Walking the Line from "100 Boots",* 1971–73. 10 photographs 9 × 12" each. Lent courtesy the artist and Ronald Feldman, Fine Arts, New York.

Stephen Antonakos. *Incomplete Pink Neon Square,* 1974. Neon tube + transformer; 3'× 3". Lent courtesy Jane Logemann and Gerry Rosen.

Richard Artschwager. *Washington Monument,* 1964. Liquitex on celotex; 47 × 26". Lent courtesy Norman Dolph.

John Baldessari. *Trying to Roll a Ball in a Straight Line from Bottom to Top and Top to Bottom (4 Photographs Per Second),* 1973. Color photographs; 110 × 5". Lent courtesy Sonnabend Gallery, NYC and the artist.

John Baldessari. *Trying to Roll a Disc in a Straight Line from Bottom to Top and Top to Bottom (4 Photographs Per Second),* 1973. Black and white photographs; 125 × 5". Lent courtesy Sonnabend Gallery, NYC and the artist.

John Baldessari. *Throwing a Ball Once to Get Three Melodies,* 1973. Book; 8 × 10". Lent Courtesy Sonnabend Gallery, NYC and the artist.

Robert Barry. *Moving Line, 0° – 350° × 50°,* 1968. Ink on paper; 8 pieces each 11 × 8.5". Lent courtesy the artist.

Robert Barry. *It is . . . It isn't . . . ,* 1972. Ink on paper; 4 pieces each 11 × 8.5". Lent courtesy the artist.

Jennifer Bartlett. *One Foot Line,* 1974. Enamel silkscreen on steel; 12 × 12". Lent courtesy Parrish Art Museum, gift Paul F. Walter.

Mel Bochner. *Seven Properties of Between,* 1971–72. Stones on paper on floor; 8½ × 110". Lent courtesy Sonnabend Gallery, NYC.

Chris Burden. *Shoot,* 1971. Photo mural; 48 × 96". Lent courtesy the artist and Ronald Feldman, Fine Arts, New York.

Christo. *Running Fence, Sonoma and Martin Counties, California,* 1972–76. Color photographs; 26¼ × 39¼". Lent courtesy the artist.

Gordon Matta-Clark. *Humphrey Street Splitting,* Englewood, New Jersey, 1974. Cibachrome photograph; 29¾ × 39½". Lent courtesy Holly and Horace Solomon.

Walter De Maria. *Las Vegas Piece,* 1969. Desert Valley (95 miles NE Las Vegas, Nevada). Photograph; 16 × 13½ × 1". Lent courtesy the artist.

Walter De Maria. *Vertical Earth Kilometer,* 1977. Photograph; 15⅜ × 16½ × 1". Lent courtesy the artist.

Dan Flavin. *Diagonal of May 25, 1963,* 1963. Edition 1/3. Blue fluorescent light; 8'. Lent courtesy Heiner Friedrich.

Henry Flynt. *Each Point on This Line is a Composition,* January 1961 (reconstruction 1981). Ink on paper; 28 × 21.6 cm. Lent courtesy The Gilbert and Lila Silverman Fluxus Collection.

Hamish Fulton. *Eleven Notches for an Eleven Day Walking Journey from the Middle to the North Coast of Tasmania,* 1979. Photograph; 10¾ × 31¾". Lent courtesy private collection.

Robert Grosvenor. *Untitled,* 1975. Wood-creosote; 8' 6 × 8 × 9". Lent courtesy Paula Cooper Gallery, NYC.

Hans Haacke. *Ice Stick,* 1966. Refrigeration unit, stainless steel, housing; 24 × 24 × 70". Lent courtesy Art Gallery of Ontario.

Michael Heizer. *Rotary Double Negative.* 1969. Photograph; 2 × 12'. Lent courtesy Xavier Fourcade, Inc.

Eva Hesse. *Untitled* (Ice Piece), 1969. Fiberglass and wire; 744 × 1". Lent courtesy Xavier Fourcade, Inc.

Nancy Holt. *Locator with Mirror,* 1972. Steel 2" I pipe; 5 × 1'. Lent courtesy John Weber Gallery, NYC.

Douglas Huebler. *The Line Represented Above These Words is Rotating at the Rate of One Revolution Per Day,* 1968–69. Typeface. Lent courtesy the artist.

Peter Hutchinson. *Continental Divide,* 1970. Print—photographs and silkscreen; 30 × 20". Lent courtesy the artist.

Patrick Ireland. *Meribah,* 1969. Ink on paper; 24 × 29". Lent courtesy Charles Cowles Gallery.

Patrick Ireland. *Untitled,* 1973. Rope, liquitex, nylon; 87 × 3/8". Lent courtesy Charles Cowles Gallery.

Robert Irwin. *Crazy Otto,* 1962. Oil on canvas; 66 × 65". Lent courtesy The Pace Gallery, NYC.

Patricia Johanson. *William Rush,* 1966. Steel painted with red lead; 8 × 200 × 1/4". Lent courtesy the artist.

Don Judd. *Untitled,* 1968. Blue lacquer on galvanized iron; 5 × 40 × 9". Lent courtesy DIA Art Foundation, NYC.

Ellsworth Kelly. *Yellow Relief,* 1955. Oil on canvas; 2 joined panels, 24 × 24". Lent courtesy the artist.

Alain Kirili. *Untitled,* 1973. Iron, 8' × 1". Lent courtesy the artist.

Rockne Krebs. *Rite de Passage,* 1971. Passage #4. Argon blue line across a darkened field adjacent to the museum into a swamp-like landscape. It was keyed to two palm trees. Photo documentation; 40 × 30". Lent courtesy the artist.

Rockne Krebs. *Rite de Passage,* 1971. Passage 1. Esplanade Avenue from the French Quarter to the statue of General Beauregard. A total distance of three miles. Photo documentation; 30 × 40". Lent courtesy the artist.

Sol Le Witt. *A Line from the Lower Left Corner to the Upper Right Corner (No. 175),* 1973. Black crayon. Lent courtesy John Weber Gallery.

Roy Lichtenstein. *Blue Seascape,* 1966. Oil and magna on canvas; 24 × 36". Lent courtesy David Lichtenstein.

Piero Manzoni. *Line 10 Meters Long,* 1959. Canister with label and fragment of a line, containing a black (ink) line on bluish paper; 8¾ × 393". Lent courtesy The Gilbert and Lila Silverman Collection.

Anthony McCall. *Line Describing a Cone* (16mm film, 1973) and *Four Projected Movements* (16mm film, 1975). Two offset printed announcement cards, each 5¾ × 8¼". Lent courtesy the artist.

John McCracken. *Untitled* (Orange Wall Relief), 1973. Fiberglass on wood; 93 × 21 × 4". Lent courtesy Robert Elkon Gallery, Inc., NYC.

Robert Morris. *Pace and Process,* 1972. Pencil on paper, 29½ × 39½". Lent courtesy Herbert Lust.

Robert Morris. *Rope Piece,* 1964 (reconstructed 1984). Rope and wood blocks; 219 × 10 × 10". Lent courtesy the artist.

Robert Murray. *Lima,* c. 1966. Steel painted red, 7½ × 91 × 13". Lent courtesy Cintra Murray.

Forrest Myers. *Laser with Diamond,* 1963. Ink on paper; 12 × 18". Lent courtesy the artist.

Forrest Myers. *Laser with Wine Glass,* 1963. Ink on paper; 12 × 18". Lent courtesy the artist.

Forrest Myers. *Laser with Speaker and Mirror,* 1963. Ink on paper; 12 × 18". Lent courtesy the artist.

Forrest Myers. *Beam Through Wall,* 1963. Ink on paper; 12 × 18". Lent courtesy the artist.

Forrest Myers. *Laser Installation,* 1963–84. Argon Laser; beam diameter 1/40" × length of gallery. Lent courtesy the artist.

Bruce Nauman. *Gauze,* 1969. Film. Lent courtesy Castelli/Sonnabend tapes and films, NYC.

Barnett Newman. *Now I,* 1965. Acrylic on canvas; 78 × 12". Lent courtesy Gerald S. Elliott.

Richard Nonas. *Chop,* 1971. Wood; 16 × 12" × 30'. Lent courtesy the artist.

Dennis Oppenheim. *Boundary Split,* 1968. St. John River; Fort Kent, Maine. Series of cuts made perpendicular to the Time Boundary—U.S.A./Canada. Gasoline powered chain saw; 4 × 4 × 25'. Lent courtesy the artist.

Dennis Oppenheim. *Dream Lines,* 1976. Project proposal for Western United States. Sprayed tar/colored dry pigments; 2000'. Lent courtesy the artist.

Dennis Oppenheim. *Time Line,* 1968. Boundary between U.S.A./Canada, St. John River; Fort Kent, Maine. 1 × 3 × 3' cut between two countries. Lent courtesy the artist.

Nam June Paik. *Zen for TV* (copy no. 4/12), 1963/75. Altered GE T.V. set; 21 × 16 × 13". Lent courtesy The Gilbert and Lila Silverman Fluxus Collection.

Beverly Pepper. *Torre Pieno Nel Vuoto,* 1969. Stainless steel; 95 × 20 × 40". Lent courtesy the artist.

Leon Polk Smith. *Constellation: Three Yellow Ovals,* 1967. Acrylic on canvas, 105 × 52". Lent courtesy Washburn Gallery, NYC.

Robert Rauschenberg. *Jackpot* (Jammer #386), 1975. Fabric and wood, 74½ × 60¼". Lent courtesy Leo Castelli Gallery.

George Rickey. *Single Line,* 1964–70. Stainless steel, marble base; 11½ × 19 × 2½". Lent courtesy Stuart Rickey.

Dorothea Rockburne. First Working Drawing for Gradient Field II, 1977. Strathmore 3-ply bond paper, vellum, sanguine and conte; 30 × 40". Lent courtesy Xavier Fourcade, Inc., NYC.

Charles Ross. *Solar Burn, Aries Day (Red),* April 10, 1979 (remake of 1971–72 original). Sunlight, wood, and painted aluminum frame; 48½ × 16". Lent courtesy John Weber Gallery.

Charles Ross. *Solar Burn, Virgo Day (Green) (Yellow-Green),* September 11, 1979 (remake of 1971 original). Sunlight, wood, painted aluminum frame; 48½ × 16". Lent courtesy John Weber Gallery.

Fred Sandback. *Untitled #80.103,* 1974. Black wool; 10' × ½". Lent courtesy DIA Foundation, Inc.

Fred Sandback. *Untitled #86L,* 1968. (One of 133 drawings for proposed construction for Heiner Friedrich Gallery, Munich [#130]). Pen and pencil on yellow legal paper; 5 × 7⅞". Lent courtesy the artist.

Fred Sandback. *Untitled #87L,* 1968. (One of 133 drawings for proposed construction for Heiner Friedrich Gallery, Munich [#131]). Pen and pencil on yellow legal paper; 5 × 7⅞". Lent courtesy the artist.

Fred Sandback. *Untitled #88L,* 1968. (One of 133 drawings for proposed construction for Heiner Friedrich Gallery, Munich [#132]). Pen and pencil on yellow legal paper; 5 × 7⅞". Lent courtesy the artist.

Fred Sandback. *Untitled,* 1968. (One of 133 drawings for proposed construction for Heiner Friedrich Gallery, Munich [#133]). Pen and pencil on yellow legal paper; 5 × 7⅞". Lent courtesy the artist.

Fred Sandback. *Untitled #91L,* 1972. (Isometric rendering of one of the "16 Variationen Von 2 Diagonalen Linien"). Chrome yellow pastel on Arches cover; 23 × 31". Lent courtesy the artist.

Fred Sandback. *Untitled #92L,* 1972. (Isometric rendering of one of the "16 Varitionen Von 2 Diagonalen Linien"). Chrome yellow pastel on Arches cover; 23 × 31". Lent courtesy the artist.

Richard Serra. *30 Feet of Rolled Lead,* n.d. Lead; 3 × 24 × 10". Lent courtesy Holly and Horace Solomon, NYC.

Alan Shields. *Rope Painting,* 1969–70. Acrylic on rope; 114 × ⅜". Lent courtesy Paula Cooper Gallery, NYC.

Robert Smithson. *Eight Unit Piece from Cayuga Salt Mine Project,* 1969. Mirrors and rock salt; 11 × 30 × 300". Lent courtesy John Weber Gallery, NYC.

Tal Streeter. *Standing Red,* 1970. Wood painted deep red; 8' × 12 × 12". Lent courtesy the artist.

Michelle Stuart. *Niagara Gorge Path Relocated,* 1975. Rocks, earth on muslin backed paper; 460' × 5'2". Lent courtesy the artist.

Michelle Stuart. *Niagara Gorge Path Relocated (detail),* 1975. Rocks, earth on muslin backed paper; 460' × 5'2". Lent courtesy the artist.

Michelle Stuart. *#26, Peterboro, New Hampshire,* 1974. Earth, rock indentations on muslin mounted on rag paper; 244 × 62". Lent courtesy the artist.

Paul Thek. *Comet,* December 24, 1973. Watercolor, ink on newspaper; 23 × 33". Lent courtesy Barbara Gladstone Gallery, NYC.

Robert Watts. *2" (2 inches),* 1964–79. Each performance of this work, which Watts performed between 1964 and 1979, was done with this ribbon. Photograph during the Flux Fest at Fluxhall; "Street Events" on Canal Street, NYC, May 23, 1964. Ben Vautier and Allison Knowles and street traffic are seen performing the work. Photo documentation by George Maciunas; ribbon 2 × 190". Lent courtesy The Gilbert and Lila Silverman Fluxus Collection.

William Wegman. *Four Panel Board Cutting Piece* ("Electric Saw"), 1973. 4 photographs each 14 × 11". Lent courtesy Holly Solomon and the artist.

Lawrence Weiner. *Overdone. Done-over. And Overdone. And Done-over.,* 1970. Language plus the material referred to. Lent courtesy Leo Castelli Gallery, NYC.

Mia Westerland. *Fiberglass Wall Piece,* 1973. Flannel soaked in polyester resin; 39½ × 25 × 2". Lent courtesy Leo Castelli Gallery, NYC.

Robert Whitman. *Untitled,* Fall 1973. Lithographs (five in series). Lent courtesy the artist.

Robert Whitman. *Untitled,* Fall 1973. Lithographs (five in series). Lent courtesy the artist.

La Monte Young. *Composition 1960; #7,* July 1960. Ink on paper; 3 × 5". Lent courtesy the artist.

La Monte Young. *Composition 1960 #10,* October 1960. 3$\frac{7}{16}$ × 8½". Lent courtesy the artist.

La Monte Young. *Composition 1960 #9,* October 1960. Envelope with card; envelope, 3¾ × 6½"; card, 3 × 5". Lent courtesy the artist.

La Monte Young. *LY 1961,* 1961. Book; Lent courtesy the artist.

Marian Zazeela. *Line of Y's #1* 31364, 1964. India ink on rice paper; 7¾ × 10⅛". Lent courtesy the artist.

Marian Zazeela. *Line of Y's #5* 42164, 1964. Graphite on black paper; 7¾ × 10⅛". Lent courtesy the artist.

Marian Zazeela. *Line of Z's #6* 42164, 1964. Graphite on black paper; 7¾ × 10⅛". Lent courtesy the artist.

Marian Zazeela. *Line of Y's and Z's #2* 31364, 1964. India ink on rice paper; 7¾ × 10". Lent courtesy the artist.

Selected Bibliography

Alloway, L. *Systematic Painting.* New York: Solomon R. Guggenheim Museum, 1966.

Arnason, H.H. *American Abstract Expressionists and Imagists.* New York: Solomon R. Guggenheim Museum, 1961.

Arnason, H.H. *History of Modern Art; Painting Sculpture, Architecture.* New York: Prentice-Hall, 1968.

Atkinson, T. and Baldwin, M. "De legius naterae." *Studio,* May 1971, 181: 226–32.

Baker, K. "Andre in Retrospect." *Art in America,* April 1980, 68:88–94.

Battcock, G. *Minimal Art: A Critical Anthology.* New York : E.P. Dutton & Co., Inc., 1968.

Battcock, G. *The New Art: A Critical Anthology.* New York: E.P. Dutton & Co., Inc., 1960.

Benedikt, M. "Sculpture As Architecture: New York Letter, 1966–67," *Art International,* Vol. IV, Nos.7, 10, and Vol. 16, Nos.1, 2, 4.

Bochner, M. "Serial Art/ Systems: Solipsism." *Arts,* Summer 1967, 41: 39–43.

Bochner, M. "The Serial Attitude." *Artforum,* December 1967, 5: 28–33.

Bonnefoi, C. "Louis Kahn and Minimalism." *Oppositions,* Spring 1981, 24: 3–25.

Brion, M. *Art Since 1945.* New York: Abrams, 1958.

Brooks, R. "Please No Slogans," *Studio,* March 1976, 191:155+.

Burnham, J. *Beyond Modern Sculpture: The Effects of Science and Technology on the Sculpture of This Century.* New York: G. Braziller, 1968.

Calas, N. and Calas, E., *Icons and Images of the Sixties.* New York: E. P. Dutton & Co., Inc., 1969.

Clay, J. "U.S.A. 'réel' place au géant, exposition de l'art moderne au Grand Palais." *Connaissance Arts,* November 1968, 201: 21+.

Dienst, R.G. "Absolute Malerie: zu einer Kunst der Reduktion und Differenzierung." *Kunstwerk,* 1981, Vol. 34, No. 4: 3–48.

Ercegovic, M. "Minimal Play [Modernism Gallery: San Francisco]." *Artweek,* September 11, 1982, 13: 7.

Foster, H. "Donald Judd, Heiner Friedrich Gallery, New York." *Artforum,* January 1979, 17: 58–59.

Fried, M. "Art and Objecthood," *Artforum,* June 1967, Vol.5 No.10: 12–23.

Geldzahler, H. *New York Painting and Sculpture: 1940–1970.* New York: Metropolitan Museum of Art, 1969.

Geldzahler, H.; Rose, B.; and Stella, F. *Shape and Structure.* New York: Tibor de Nagy Gallery, 1965.

Goossen, E.C. *Eight Young Artists.* New York: Hudson River Museum, 1964.

Goossen, E.C. *The Art of the Real.* New York: Museum of Modern Art, 1968.

Graham, D. "Art in Relation to Architecture; Architecture in Relation to Art." *Artforum,* February 1979, 17: 22–29.

Greenberg, C. "Avant-Garde Attitudes: New Art in the Sixties," *Studio International,* April 1970, 179: 142–145.

Griffiths, P. *Modern Music: The Avant-Garde Since 1945.* New York: G. Braziller, 1981.

Halley, P. "Beat, Minimalists, New Wave, and Robert Smithson." *Art,* May 1981, 55: 120–121.

Heller, B. *Toward a New Abstraction.* New York: The Jewish Museum, 1963.

Henry G. "New York Letter." *Art International,* May 1971, 15: 73–74+.

Honnef, K. "Absage an die Asthetik der Minimal Art." *Architecture,* May/June 1983, 13: 60–61.

Hunter, S. and Jacubus, J. *American Art and Architecture of the Twentieth Century.* New York: Prentice-Hall, 1974.

Johnson, T. "The Original Minimalists." *Village Voice,* July 27, 1982, Vol. 27, No. 30: 70.

Judd, D. "Specific Objects." *Arts Yearbook 8,* 1965, 74–82.

Kardon, J. *Line.* Philadelphia: Visual Arts Museum, Philadelphia College of Art, 1976.

Kirby M. *The Art of Time: Essays on the Avant-Garde.* New York: E.P. Dutton & Co., Inc., 1969.

Kramer, H. "Episodes From the Sixties." *Art in America,* January-February 1970, 58: 56–61.

Krauss, R. "Sense and Sensibility, Reflection on Post '60s Sculpture." *Artforum,* November 1973, 12: 43–53.

Kuspit, D.B. "Postminimalism." *Art Journal,* Summer 1979, Vol. 38, No.4: 298–300.

Lebeer, P. "Le Minimal Art ou le Rasoir d'Occam." *XX[e] Siecle,* December 1973, No. 41: 141–145.

Lippard, L. and Develing, E. *Minimal Art.* The Hague: Gemeentemuseum, March 23–May 26, 1968.

Lippard, L. *Six Years of the Dematerialization of the Art Object From 1966–1972.* New York: Praeger Publishers, 1975.

Lippard, L. "The Third Stream Constructed Paintings and Painted Structures." *Artforum,* Spring 1965, 4: 45–49.

Lucie-Smith, E. *Late Modern: The Visual Arts Since 1945.* New York: Praeger Publishers, 1976.

McShine, K. *Primary Structures.* New York: The Jewish Museum, 1966.

Meelson, P. "Art as Symbol of Thing." *British Journal Aesthetics,* Winter 1981,Vol. 21, No. 1: 22–31.

Morris, R. "Aligned with Narca." *Artforum,* October 1975, 14: 26–39.

Morrum, R. "Notes on Sculpture." *Artforum,* Part I, February 1966, Vol. 4, No. 6: 42–44; Part II, October 1966, Vol. 5, No. 2: 20–23.

Muller, G. and Gorgoni, G. *The New Avant-Garde: Issues for the Art of the Seventies.* New York: Praeger Publishers, 1972.

Pelligrino, A. *New Tendencies in Art.* New York: Crown Publishers, 1966.

Philip, L. "Literalism and Abstraction: Frank Stella's Retrospective at the Modern." *Artforum,* April 1970, 8: 44–51.

Prokopoff, S. "Logic of Vision." *Arts,* September 1974, 49: 45–47.

Prweski, A. "Artificial Paradise." *Art and Artists,* April 1969, 4: 50–53.

Pugh, S. "Towards a Minimal Art." *Studio,* January 1972, 183: 23–25.

Reichardt, J. "Extreme as a Virtue." *Art Digest,* 1973, Vol. 43, No. 16: 675.

Rickey, G. *Constructivism: Origins and Evolution.* New York: G. Braziller, 1967.

Rose, B. "Looking at American Sculpture." *Artforum,* February 1965, Vol. 3, No. 5: 29–36.

Rose, B. "The Politics of Art, Part II." *Artforum,* January 1969, 7: 44–49.

Rose, B. "ABC Art." *Art in America,* October-November 1965, 53: 56–69.

Rubin, W. "Younger American Painters." *Art International,* Zurich, 1960, Vol. IV, No. 1: 24–31.

Salamon, A. *The New Art Scene.* New York: Holt, Rinehart, and Winston, 1967.

Sandler, I. *Concrete Expressionism.* New York: The Loeb Student Center, April 1965.

Sandler, I. "The New Cool Art." *Art in America,* February 1965, 53: 96–101.

Sandler, I. and Rose, B. "Sensibility of the Sixties." *Art in America,* January-February 1967, 55: 44–57.

Schwartz, S. "Little Big Sculpture." *Art in America,* March 1976, 64: 53–55.

Seitz, W. "Contemporary Sculpture, Arts Yearbook," *Art Digest,* 1965, No. 8.

Tillim, S. "Scale and the Future of Modernism." *Artforum,* October 1967, Vol. 6, No. 2: 14–18.

Tuchman, M. *American Sculpture of the Sixties.* Los Angeles: Los Angeles County Museum of Art, April 28-June 25, 1967.

Tuchman, P. *Minimal Art.* Madrid: Jues March Foundation, January-March 1981.

Tuchman, P. "Minimalism and Critical Response." *Artforum,* May 1977, 15: 26–30.

Tuchman, P. "Minimalism: The Art of the Interesting." *The Michigan Quarterly Review,* Summer 1981, 20: 210–223.

Van der Marck, J. *American Art Third Quarter Century.* Seattle: Seattle Art Museum, 1973.

Varian, E. *Schenata 7.* New York: Finch College Museum of Art, 1967.

Waldman, D. "Holding the Floor." *Art News,* October 1970, 69: 60–62+.

Weschler, L. "Lines of Inquiry [Robert Irwin's Minimalist Paintings]." *Art in America,* March 1982, 70: 102–109.

Wolheim, R. "Minimal Art." *Arts Magazine,* January, 39: 26–32.

Young, L. *An Anthology.* New York: Maciunas, 1963.